THE COMPLETE GUIDE TO

LOG AND CEDAR HOMES

Also by Gary D. Branson:

The Complete Guide to Barrier-Free Housing
The Complete Guide to Floors, Walls, and Ceilings
The Complete Guide to Lumber Yards and Home Centers
The Complete Guide to Manufactured Housing
The Complete Guide to Recycling at Home
The Complete Guide to Remodeling Your Basement

THE COMPLETE GUIDE TO

LOG AND CEDAR HOMES

All About Buying, Building, Decorating, and Furnishing Log, Cedar, and Post & Beam Homes

Gary D. Branson

BETTERWAY BOOKS
Cincinnati, Ohio

Prepress services by Studio 500 Associates

97 96 95 94 93   5 4 3 2 1

Library of Congress Cataloging-in-Publication Data

Branson, Gary D.
    The complete guide to log and cedar homes : all about buying, building, decorating, and furnishing log, cedar, and post & beam homes / Gary D. Branson. — 1st ed.
        p.   cm.
    Includes index.
    ISBN 1-55870-276-8 : $16.95
    1. Log cabins. 2. Cedar. I. Title.
TH4840.B72 1993
690'.837—dc20
                                                                          92-38664
                                                                               CIP

For my sister, Wilma Clark, who introduced me to "Vagabond's House."

Acknowledgments

We would like to acknowledge the cooperation and contributions of the National Association of Home Builders (NAHB) and the Log Homes Council; Lindal Cedar Homes; Timberpeg; Appalachian Log Homes; Perma-Chink Systems Inc.; Rocky Mountain Timber Products; Amerlink, the Wood Heating Alliance (WHA); Heat-n-Glo Fireplace Products, Inc.

Contents

Introduction

Home, according to Carl Sandburg, is the place that, when you go there, they have to take you in. The word "home" has a special meaning to me because my entire working life has been involved with building, remodeling, or writing about housing. My occupational leaning towards involvement with shelter could be hereditary. A distant relative, who did a "Roots"-type study of the Branson family tree, relates that those of our forebears who were not farmers were likely to be carpenters and builders. Since my father also was in the housing business and taught building trades to both my brother and me, I am quite sure that the business is in my blood and genes.

When Europeans first stumbled upon this continent, the terrain was 40 percent forest, 40 percent prairies, and 20 percent mountains and deserts. Because our forefathers made landfall along the heavily-forested eastern coast, and because wood construction was common in the northern European countries from which the early immigrants came, the early shelters were built of readily available wood, an abundant and easy to work resource. Note that these first shelters were not fancy log houses; rather they were crude huts. Log homes came later, in the 1600's.

The early immigrants reached these shores via wooden ships, and the maintenance crews were called "shipwrights" or "boatwrights." The early houses built in America were built by these ships' carpenters, so one also finds a heavy emphasis on ship-type, post and beam timber construction in the original colonies. It would be decades before sawmills were built to mill logs and timber and turn it into cut lumber for wood frame construction such as we have today.

Because of our history, and the linking of the log cabin with our heroes to show that they were men of the people (Abraham Lincoln was called "the Great Commoner"), Americans have had a historic love affair with log and timber homes. And, although log homes are today much in the minority in new home construction, the past two decades have seen a tremendous growth and renewed interest in construction of log and timber homes. Today, however, these rustic all-wood homes are no longer poor man's shelter, but are usually middle to upper bracket in cost and are no longer considered shelter for the financially limited. They combine the rustic beauty of the wood home with today's building technology to yield a home that may be the ultimate in livability.

While visiting my brother recently, I was telling him of some of my current projects and mentioned that I was doing a book on log and timber housing. He replied "You know, I always wanted to build a log house. When I can't get to sleep, I start to build my log house in my mind. Usually, I don't get beyond the foundation before I fall asleep, but I've always dreamed ..." The appeal of log and timber houses is virtually universal. Many or most of us have felt the urge to build a log or timber home. Again, we have historical and ancestral ties to the concept of log homes: my grandfather, Tillman

Branson, and his sister, Lillian Branson, each homesteaded a quarter-section of land (160 acres) in the Cherokee Strip in 1893, á la the Tom Cruise movie, *Far and Away*, and built their first homes from logs cut along Bitter Creek, near Enid, Oklahoma.

Our predominantly European ancestry and experiences influence us towards houses made of wood; wood that is prominent and visible. Contrary to popular belief, the early immigrants did not build log houses, but lived in crude dugouts or "wigwams." The German and Scandinavian settlers who arrived in America around 1638 built the first saddle-notched log homes. Because the forest needed to be cleared so it could be farmed and the people needed housing, the log houses became the logical and preferred home as the early settlers poured into the East and the South. With the materials so readily available and the simple style of log house construction, a log house could be raised in a single day.

So strong was the identification of the log house with moral rectitude that politicians began to claim their right to office based on their humble but virtuous beginnings. Our ninth president, William Henry Harrison, ran as the Log Cabin Candidate in his presidential election, even though he was raised on a great plantation in Virginia. (Harrison had lived briefly in a log cabin while in the army.) Indeed, when our sixteenth president, Abraham Lincoln, ran for president in 1860, being born in a log cabin was viewed as an indication of moral superiority. He was claimed as a man of the people — "The Great Commoner"— who was born in a log cabin on the frontier of Kentucky. If you travel south of Louisville, Kentucky on Interstate Highway 65, or south from Lexington, Kentucky on Interstate Highway 75, it's worth a short detour to see the Lincoln Homestead at Knob Creek Farm near Bardstown, Kentucky.

In this century, the Roosevelt administration helped spread the gospel of log houses when federal agencies employed out-of-work laborers to build log lodges, bridges, ranger stations, and fire lookout towers in our national forests. In many states where lumbering is a primary industry, you will see great examples of log construction in parks and in historical centers and museums built to showcase the history of the logging industry. In my own state of Minnesota, there are fine examples of log building at the Forest History Center in Grand Rapids, Minnesota.

There is a mystique to log and timber houses, an appeal and a dream quality that endures even though our dreams of living in the all-wood house may never become reality. The catalogs for log and timber home builders often have references to the fact that these are, in fact, dream books. Only a small percentage of us may actually ever live in a log or timber house. Most of us have opted, because of the choices offered and the limitations of our pocketbooks, to live in a more familiar style of housing when it actually comes time to build. Our suburban colonials and split levels and ranch houses conform to our ideas of what an urban house should be. The beauty of all-wood log houses or timber houses, set on city streets or suburban cul-de-sacs, might be in stark contrast with our "little boxes made of ticky-tack." But log houses are changing in appearance, design, and style. Today, nine out of ten log houses are built as primary residences, not as vacation retreats. And they are increasingly built in outer-ring suburbs, where they fit in just fine with the wood-sided tract-built houses. There is an ambience of nostalgia, warmth, and beauty about log and timber houses that no other building material can quite match.

Whatever form or fashion your dream house may take, we hope you enjoy our tour of log and timber homes. May you always have a very special place to call home; and when you go there, may they always take you in.

1.
Log Home Buyers' Profile

When I have a house ... as I sometime may ...
I'll suit my fancy in every way.
I'll fill it with things that have caught my eye
In drifting from Iceland to Molokai.
It won't be correct or in period style
But ... oh, I've thought for a long, long while
Of all the corners and all the nooks,
Of all the bookshelves and all the books,
The great big table, the deep soft chairs
And the Chinese rug at the foot of the stairs ...

The thought of log and timber houses may conjure up movie and television images of Davy Crockett, Dan'l Boone, or Abe Lincoln, of backwoods (and perhaps backwards) living, of that ultimate self-sufficient do-it-yourselfer, the trapper or the mountain man plying his solitary trade in the "high lonesome" reaches of the Rockies or the Blue Ridge Mountains. This image may have had some legitimacy in the past, but the times they are a' changin'. As *Professional Builder* magazine has pointed out, log homes are no longer just "little houses in the big woods."

Log homes in America had their beginnings as basic frontier housing, but by the end of the 19th century, massive log structures had become trendy vacation retreats for the upper classes. These log lodges dotted the Adirondack Mountain range in the late 1800's, and were fashionable vacation retreats for

the wealthy New York City elite. Great log lodges, designed by professional architects, were — and still are — a common sight in the forests of northern tier states along the Canadian/U.S. border, as well as in southern and western areas.

During the high unemployment years of the 1930's Depression, the United States government employed thousands of young men in the Civilian Conservation Corps (CCC) to build lookout towers, bridges, lodges, and ranger stations of logs. These log structures were built in every forest state in the nation, and tourists enjoyed their rustic beauty as they traveled the nation and visited national parks.

During the protest era of the 1960's and '70's, there was a "back to nature" movement that proposed to "drop out" of mainstream America and go native. One of the fastest growing consumer magazines of the late '70's was *Mother Earth News*, a back-to-basics periodical that preached the gospel of living simply. In 1978, Doris Muir started the *Log Home Guide* for buyers and builders of log homes. Everything old was new again: the advocates of this philosophy proposed to live on an acreage or a homestead, burning wood for energy. They would, in the manner of Henry David Thoreau, go to the woods with a borrowed axe and "cut down some tall, arrowy white pines, still in their youth, for timber," to build a house at Walden Pond. The back-to-the-land movement rediscovered the log house, and the

This model shows the traditional style many people expect when thinking of log homes.
Courtesy of Gastineau Log Homes, Inc.

This contemporary interior shows off the beauty of the log walls.
Courtesy of Gastineau Log Homes, Inc.

increasing awareness of the beauty and durability of log homes spread throughout the general population. Dozens of new companies were formed to fill the demand for pre-cut log home kits. The appeal of log homes has spread — today it is worldwide.

Today, nine out of ten log houses in the U.S. are built as the family's primary residence, not as a vacation retreat; and they are built in outer rim suburbs, not along lake shores or deep in the piney woods. In the past, most log houses were built as family do-it-yourself projects. Most of today's log houses are not built by the owners: the majority of log houses are completely turn-key affairs built by professional distributors or contractors.

The demand for log houses is not by any means limited to the U.S. If you study the membership list of the Log Homes Council (LHC) in the Appendix, you will see that many of these companies sell log houses worldwide. An estimated 1,500 log houses will be sold to Japan alone in 1992. Other log house customers are found in Canada, England, the Far East, the Middle East, Europe, and Korea. The appeal of log houses is universal.

Who buys log houses, and what are the deciding factors that guide them in these important decisions? We have an accurate profile of the American log home buyer, taken from a survey conducted by the Log Homes Council. It may surprise many of us to learn that the average log home buyers are young (between twenty-five and forty-five years of age); are married with children; have some college education; work as managers or professionals; and have a household income of about $40,000 per year. For many or most buyers, the log home represents upward mobility: most log home buyers have owned conventionally-built houses in the past.

There are about 25,000 log homes built annually in the United States. About one in every thirteen custom-built homes is of log construction. Most log home companies now manufacture the logs; i.e., the logs are milled so they are peeled and bark-free, uniform in diameter, and shaped with tongue-and-groove edges to ensure tight-fitting, weather-resistant joints. In addition to the members of the Log Homes Council, there are hundreds of independent log builders who hand-craft the logs and fit them individually at the job site.

LOG HOME LIFESTYLES

Log homes are available in almost any desired architectural style. Most manufacturers will send a catalog showing their stock log home plans, but the homes can be redesigned to fit the needs of the buyer. An evening spent browsing through a log home catalog will reveal log plans in almost any configuration. There are A-frames, Scandinavian chalets, two stories, and ranch homes. The style may be the ultimate in rustic living, or built with D-logs so the interior side of the walls is flat and contemporary in style. What are some other attributes that buyers discover in log houses?

Low Maintenance

Log houses are noted for their low maintenance, interior and exterior. Conventional log construction means no painting or papering, no cracks to patch, and less time devoted to interior repairs. The log home exterior should not be painted. Ordinary house paints will crack and peel as the logs expand and shrink with the weather. Instead, a staining or transparent wood treatment provides protection, and only needs occasional cleaning and recoating. If you don't want to spend your life studying paint charts, an alternative might be to consider building a log house.

Energy Efficiency

In Chapter 2, Advantages of Log and Timber Homes, we discuss at length the reasons log houses are superior to ordinary stick-built houses in energy efficiency. The increased thermal mass of log houses will put the owner in the forefront of the environmental movement when it comes to energy-efficient construction. A ten-year joint study conducted by the construction industry, the U.S. Departments of Energy (DOE) and Housing and Urban Development (HUD), and the National Bureau of Standards shows that log or solid wood construction can save up to 25 percent on annual energy (heating and cooling) bills when compared to stick-built or ordinary frame construction.

Flexibility

Modern log construction and design techniques can produce a log house that will fit into any setting, from mountaintop retreat to sophisticated urban site. The customer can design the home of his or her dreams, to fit any lifestyle. Many or most log home companies offer custom-design services, including computer-aided design (CAD). Are you young, with a growing family? Build with room for expansion, or select a plan that easily allows for addition of another wing later. If your family includes an elderly or disabled person, plan a barrier-free design for greater accessibility.

Tradition

There is a traditional appeal connected with log houses. The early waves of immigrants to this country came from northern Europe, where forests were extensive and log houses were the common (and the commoner's) abode. The eastern and northern portions of the U.S. were very much like the countries these immigrants came from, not only in the vast and seemingly endless forests, but also in the weather extremes of the four seasons. The early settlers knew that log houses provided the most snug and comfortable shelters from winter cold and summer heat. Today's log houses combine that log heritage with modern technology to offer houses that fit any lifestyle and blend into any setting.

Economy/Investment

Log houses are not cheap to build. One source estimates the cost of pre-cut log house kits at between $50 and $75 per square foot, and the cost of hand-crafted log houses at about $100 per square foot. When considering catalog prices for log home kits, remember that the finished cost will be at least double, and perhaps triple, the cost of the kit. These prices are decidedly upscale when measured against conventional construction costs. In light of these upscale prices, we may ask: does log construction cost, or does it pay?

Longevity is one basis for the economy of log houses. A log house will last for many generations, even hundreds of years, if it receives basic minimum maintenance. Log houses do not need expensive and time-consuming interior and exterior maintenance, and are among the few home choices that actually have appreciated in value throughout these years of stagnant housing prices. Many owners have estimated that their log houses were worth double their actual price on the day they turned the key in the door. In many cases, actual buy offers back up these claims.

But low maintenance and high return on investment are not the only economic advantages. Throw in the already discussed superior energy efficiency (see Chapter 2), and you will have more than enough convincing reasons a growing number of people are choosing log and timber houses over conventional construction.

Case Histories

In a brochure titled "An American Dream: The Log Home," the Log Home Council profiles a number of families who have chosen log homes. A short review of these case histories reveals the motivation of those who live in log homes.

Case #1: A New England Salt Box. Tim and Fran G. did not build their log home; they purchased it from the original owner. As they approached their marriage date nearly two years ago, Tim and Fran went house-hunting. It was Fran who found the 2,400-square-foot house, but both fell in love with it. Built on the Maine coast, the house has four bedrooms, a living room with a 25-foot ceiling, and a huge Russian-style fireplace that provides virtually all the heat for the house. A large deck overlooks the ocean. Energy-efficient windows in every room also provide a view of the Atlantic. What's not to like?

Case #2: Contemporary Chalet. Warren and Diane B. chose their chalet-style home for what Diane calls "an uptown look." The chalet features a full glass front and an open floor plan to complement their mountainside lot in Townville, South Carolina. The chalet is built in a "T" shape: the master

A charming traditional-style great room.
Courtesy of Gastineau Log Homes, Inc.

Open construction is one of the charms of many log homes.
Courtesy of Gastineau Log Homes, Inc.

Log construction sets off beautiful antique wood furniture in this bedroom.
Courtesy of Gastineau Log Homes, Inc.

The traditional chinked exterior is a rustic background for the welcoming front porch
of this log home. Courtesy of Appalachian Log Homes.

edroom is secluded in one wing of the "T", the secondary bedrooms in the opposite wing, with the living area in the center. The master bedroom suite has conventional 8-foot wallboard ceilings, dressing rooms, a walk-in closet, and a whirlpool tub. The furnishings are contemporary, not rustic; the results are fabulous.

Case #3: Country Rustic. Building a 5,600-square-foot log home that includes a second floor loft, a full basement and recreation room, a double garage, and a massive fireplace that contains 21 tons of Tennessee fieldstone is just a walk on the beach for a fellow who builds and flies his own airplanes, owns and operates a combination auto parts/hardware store, and raises cattle as a sideline. Gary and Sue A. had dreamed of a country log home for twenty-five years, and the dream took wing when a friend began to build his log home. After talking to the friend, they approached his manufacturer and worked out their own design. Building the home took eleven months; four months of that was spent building the massive walk-through fireplace and chimney. The fireplace was designed by Gary: engineers told him it couldn't be done. (But then, according to engineering principles, bumblebees can't fly.) The happy homeowners live five miles outside the city limits of Adairsville, Georgia.

Case #4: "Little House on the Prairie." Brad and Cheryl K. live in the log house he built during his bachelor days. They remodeled it since they married: they doubled the floor space, including a log dog house for their pet. Cheryl prizes the energy efficiency and modern living the log house offers, while it preserves a nostalgic air. Home for the little house is Eugene, Oregon.

Case #5: An American Prairie Cottage. The exterior is that of an old-fashioned log home; the interior is strictly modern. Michael and Carolyn H. built the 3,000 square-foot house with a great room, kitchen, dining room, study, full bath, and sunroom on the first floor. Upstairs are three bedrooms and two baths. The master bedroom has a balcony that overlooks the sunroom below. The interior partitions are wallboard, so Carolyn used wall coverings extensively to expand the modern feel of the home's interior. The cottage is right at home in Belvidere, Illinois.

As you can see, the types of log homes possible are as varied as the families who live in them. Are you a potential customer for a log home? Only you can decide. In Chapter 4, Choosing the Log or Timber Home, we will try to help you make your decision.

2.
Advantages of Log and Timber Homes

My house will stand on the side of a hill
By a slow broad river, deep and still,
With a tall lone pine on guard nearby
Where the birds can sing and the storm winds cry.
A flagstone walk with lazy curves
Will lead to the door where a Pan's head serves
As a knocker there like a vibrant drum
To let me know that a friend has come,
And the door will squeak as I swing it wide
To welcome you to the cheer inside ...

Over the years, a number of misconceptions have arisen regarding the qualities of log homes. One common misconception became the subject of heated (no pun intended) debate in the early days of the 1970's oil shortages. The misconception was that log homes were not as energy efficient as were the stick-built, framed, and insulated homes.

THE QUESTION OF ENERGY EFFICIENCY

The evolving interest in increasing the energy efficiency of housing led to efforts by the housing industry and by governmental agencies to find a way to categorize home construction according to its energy efficiency. Thus arose the ranking of insulation (and other types of building material) by its "R-factor," or potential resistance to heat loss. As these R-factors were being measured and developed, the log or solid wood home was assigned a very low R-factor, when compared to the stick-built home with its 2 x 4 framing and fiberglass insulation. For example, the R-factor for pine logs is calculated at R = 1.18 per inch of thickness. In a study by the National Bureau of Standards, which compared energy efficiency of various types of construction, a log house with walls built of 7-inch diameter solid wood logs was assigned a nominal R-10, as compared to an assigned value of around R-12 for 2 x 4 frame walls built with 3½-inch thick fiberglass batts.

The Log Home Industry Rebuttal

I first became aware of this "battle of the R's" when I was the senior editor at a home magazine called *The Family Handyman*, back in the energy conservation period of the late '70's. Doris Muir, who at that time was editor of *Muir's Log Home Guide*, had become involved in the battle over R-factors as they were being assigned to various types of residential construction. Muir's stance, if memory serves, was that: (1) the entire concept of the R-factor was flawed, because log homes were known (by their owners and boosters) to be snug and comfortable, regardless of the R-factor assigned to them. Log homes thus would "outperform their R-factors." (2) Material R-factors were the result of tests done in very controlled laboratory conditions, where little temperature variation was present, and that the laboratory test results did not duplicate the "real life" conditions that a house would experience in service. In cold conditions, stick-built housing with ordinary fiberglass insulation would underperform its R-factor, i.e., be less energy efficient than its rating would indicate. (3) In any realistic test setting, testing actual weather conditions, log homes would outperform their R-factors and would be proven to be more energy efficient than stick-built, insulated housing.

I learned that Ms. Muir was one who was quite unshakeable in her convictions, and it has been proven over time that her opinions were in fact true. Only recently (August 5, 1992) the *Minneapolis Star Tribune* newspaper carried a story stating that a major manufacturer of fiberglass insulation was being legally challenged for false claims for the energy efficiency of its insulation products. The insulation company contends that if its products are evaluated only during the coldest winter weather (in Minnesota, where the suit was raised), it probably would not meet the state's new energy standards; but if calculations were measured over an entire heating season, the insulation would comply with state standards for energy efficiency or R-factors.

In 1982, extensive tests were run by the U.S. Commerce Department's National Bureau of Standards, comparing the energy efficiency of various types of residential construction. The NBS actually built six buildings, all the same size and heated/cooled in like manner, and tested the energy consumption of these six buildings. The North American Log Homes Council has a brochure that reports the results of those NBS tests, titled "Research Report on Energy Efficiency of Log Buildings." The results clearly show the log home to be superior in energy performance, even though the insulated frame building had a perceived R-factor that was 17 percent higher than that assigned to the log building. The following may help to explain why the R-factor approach is not a reliable indicator of a building's energy performance, and why the log home in many ways outperforms its framed and insulated competitors. No matter whether you intend to build a new home, or whether that planned home will be of log or frame

construction, it is important to understand the concept and limitations of the R-factor.

UNDERSTANDING THE R-FACTOR

Although my state of Minnesota is now challenging insulation companies to substantiate their claims of cold weather R-values, I do not believe that the dispute is due to any attempt on the part of the insulation manufacturers to mislead the government or the public. Instead, I feel that the disagreement is due in great part to a misunderstanding of the concept of R-values and how that concept has gained widespread acceptance.

Developed to Measure Energy Efficiency

When the energy crunch developed in the 1970's, the governments at all levels — local, state, and federal — put pressure on material companies to establish some type of energy efficiency measurement that could be incorporated into building codes. Insulation products were tested in laboratories, under constant temperature conditions; their resistance to heat flow was measured, and a value assigned to that resistance. That assigned value was called the R-factor, or the *resistance* of the material to heat loss. Note that these tests were not conducted with the insulation "in service," or under actual weather conditions, but in laboratories that did not — could not — include all weather variables.

Energy Areas

Charts were then drawn up which split the U.S. into five different energy or "R-factor" areas. These five areas or divisions were drawn according to the various seasonal temperature extremes experienced in the country. Obviously, energy requirements were different in the southern coastal areas of Florida and Texas than in the north-central prairie states of Minnesota and the Dakotas. Still, I personally believe, after some years of study of the matter, that the zone concept for R-factors is seriously flawed.

The thermal wrap or energy efficiency standards for a structure's exterior shell should be established according to temperature extremes of both hot and

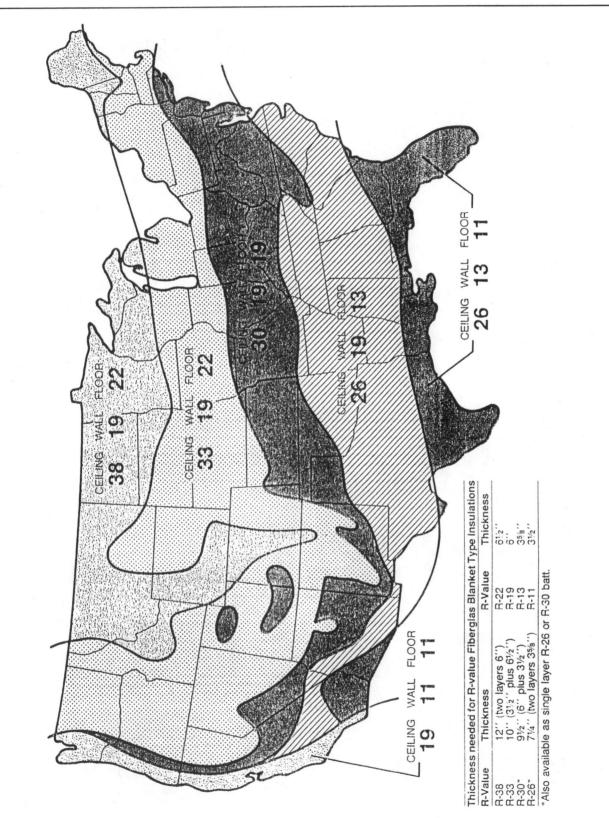

Thickness needed for R-value Fiberglas Blanket Type Insulations			
R-Value	Thickness	R-Value	Thickness
R-38	12″ (two layers 6″)	R-22	6½″
R-33	10″ (3½″ plus 6½″)	R-19	6″
R-30*	9½″ (6″ plus 3½″)	R-13	3⅝″
R-26*	7¼″ (two layers 3⅝″)	R-11	3½″
*Also available as single layer R-26 or R-30 batt.			

R-values recommended for geographic areas of the continental U.S.
Courtesy of Owens-Corning Fiberglas Corp.

An impressive exterior featuring multi-level decks.
Courtesy of Appalachian Log Homes.

A wooded setting frames this non-traditional log home exterior.
Courtesy of Appalachian Log Homes.

cold, not for cold weather alone. The energy consumption of a house in the South may in fact be greater than the energy consumption of a like house built in the North; the only difference being that, in the South, the largest percentage of energy is used to cool the interior of the house, while most of the energy consumed for the northern house is used for heating the space. For example, it would be difficult to demonstrate the rationale for having lower R-value recommendations for ceilings in my home state of Kansas, where it can be brutally cold in winter and where summer temperatures often rise above 100 degrees, than in my adopted home state of Minnesota, where prolonged cold weather can occur in winter, but where summer temperatures require less energy for air conditioning. Yet the chart shows a recommendation of R-38 for ceilings in Minnesota, but only R-30 for ceilings in Kansas. If you are building a house in an area where there are wide temperature extremes, or where heating and/or air conditioning costs are a significant factor in your annual household budget, build in all the R-factor you can. R-factors really were established according to financial considerations; i.e., the R-factor reflects the "point of no return" where added insulation cannot be justified by projected financial savings. One of several problems with this approach is that energy costs will certainly rise with annual inflation rates as well as rising in reaction to developing scarcities and shortages. Thus, recommended R-factors will change with the passing years, going up as energy costs increase.

Regional Considerations

But we must keep in mind that there are local and regional considerations that can affect the desired R-factor value. While I was an editor at *Handyman* magazine, I was assigned to write a story on "energy rip-offs." In pursuit of this story, I sent a form letter to the attorneys general of all fifty states, asking: "What advice would you give to your state's residents for avoiding rip-offs on energy-related products?" I remember to this day the replies of two of the attorneys-general. The first reply, which I promptly adopted as Branson's Rule #3, was from the attorney general for the state of Ohio. His

advice: If a claim seems to be too good to be true, it probably is neither good nor true.

The second reply, from the attorney general for the state of Hawaii, opened my eyes to what might have been obvious. In some areas, where the temperature is benign — and stable — year round, R-factors are irrelevant. In San Diego, California, or in Honolulu, Hawaii, the daily temperatures are so comfortable and so stable that home energy consumption is simply not a factor. What did the attorney general of Hawaii list as the most common energy complaint of his state's citizens? It seems that the mynah birds had discovered the fiberglass bits made a warm nest; the mynah birds would steal the fiberglass insulation from attics if the attics were not sealed so as to be absolutely mynah-proof. The point is that my experience was that R-factors should be uniform — and high — for any area that experiences any wide fluctuations of temperature, either hot or cold; and having five separate zone requirements for R-factors was in fact unnecessary and needlessly confusing to most consumers.

Other Important Factors

The various state and local building codes have adopted the R-factor as a measurement of thermal efficiency, and require specific R-factors for walls, ceilings, and floors of new houses. As stated, those required R-values vary in the five different zones established by the government. But the Home Manufacturers Council points out that while most professionals recognize R-factors to be accurate measurements of a material's thermal performance under conditions of constant interior and exterior temperatures, other factors, including temperature differential (between interior and exterior areas) and the mass of the structure, can also affect the thermal performance of a structure.

VARIABLES IN R-FACTORS

One variable that is not dealt with in the usual consideration of R-factors is that certain laws of thermodynamics are at work. These laws make R-factors less than totally accurate gauges of thermal efficiency.

Air Movement

Air movement — infiltration or exfiltration — can have an impact on the energy efficiency of a wall, floor, or ceiling. For example, suppose you build a 2 x 6-framed wall that has R-19 insulation batts, but you leave unsealed cracks around sill plates and electrical outlet boxes, and uncaulked door and window trim. The entrance or infiltration of cold air, and the exit or exfiltration of heated/air conditioned air, will make the space uncomfortable and expensive to heat or cool, no matter how high the R-values of the wall insulation.

Cracks in Log Homes

In log homes, the cracks between the logs were once a critical point of air infiltration. For today's log homes, a number of barriers are established to eliminate air infiltration. Among these is shaping logs so that they fit tightly together. Most logs today are manufactured or shaped so that the edges fit together in some sort of tongue-and-groove match joint. Also, as the log structure is assembled, the joints between each pair of logs are often filled with an insulation blanket of fiberglass or other material, then sealed with silicone caulk. Finally, the outside line (and usually the inside line) of the log joints is often filled with chinking material. The chinking material serves a dual purpose: it provides a seal against air infiltration and offers a decorative effect in the contrast between the wood logs and the chinked joint.

Other Thermodynamic Laws

Other factors that can affect and upset R-factor results include an entire bevy of thermodynamic laws. These laws are:

1. Heat always moves to cold.

2. Heat movement is omni-directional, not up: hot air rises, heat escapes wherever it can. This means that heat will escape upward, outward, or downward, depending on the insulation value of the

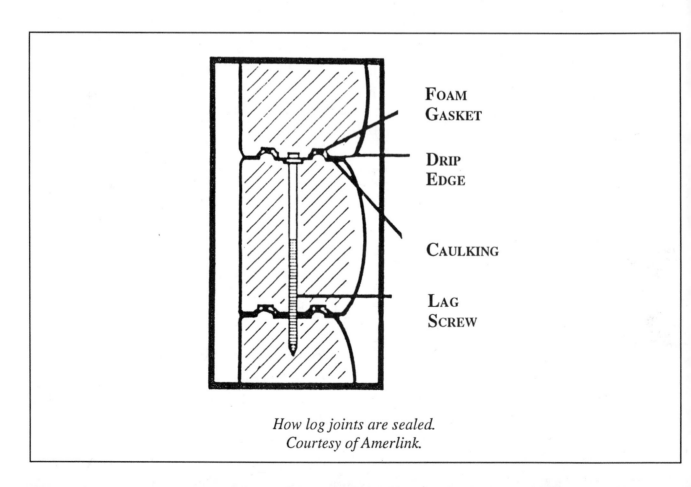

FOAM
GASKET

DRIP
EDGE

CAULKING

LAG
SCREW

How log joints are sealed.
Courtesy of Amerlink.

surfaces it contacts. If ceilings are well insulated but walls are not, the heat will flow out through the walls; if the walls are insulated but floors are not, heat escape will be downward through the floors. It is nonsense to believe that you can offset poor wall insulation by adding more ceiling insulation. To prove the fallacy of that belief (which has been extended by some insulation companies, as well as the federal government), try putting on two hats to warm your cold feet. The effect is the same. The problem of establishing a thermal barrier is like the strength of a chain, and your thermal barrier is no more effective than its weakest link. Heat will flow to cold through any avenue available.

3. The speed or rate at which heat flows to cold is not constant: the greater the differential between indoor and outdoor temperatures, the faster the rate of heat flow. For example, if the interior temperature of the house is 70 degrees, and the outdoor temperature is 60 degrees, flow of heat outward is slow, because the temperature differential between interior and exterior is small. But if the interior temperature is 70 degrees, and the outdoor temperature is zero degrees, the heat loss rate is much faster. This law is one of the conclusions reinforced by our illustrations. During warmer spring/fall weather, the log building used 46 percent less energy than the insulated wood frame building. During the winter heating season, when the temperature differential between indoors and outdoors was greater, rate of heat loss from both structures was about equal, and both used about the same energy.

4. Finally, another factor in heat loss from a building is the speed at which cold air is moving over the exterior siding. That is why energy costs go up during windy weather. It is also the reason most farmsteads retain or plant a windbreak of trees on the northerly side of the house, to shelter the house from winter winds.

THE ROLE OF MASS IN BUILDING PERFORMANCE

Architects and builders have always understood that one factor plays a very important role in the performance of a wall or a building. That factor is mass. The term mass relates to the weight, the rigidity, and the density and thickness of the wall. The greater the mass, the better the performance characteristics of the wall.

Soundproofing

Performance characteristics include the soundproofing, fireproofing, and thermal or heat-loss qualities of the wall. A heavy wall with high mass and rigidity cannot be put into vibration with sound waves, and so is much more resistant to sound transfer. A house with high-mass walls will be a quieter house, and will resist sound transfer both between interior spaces and from the exterior into the interior of the structure. Note also that increasing the size of the logs with which you build increases the mass of the walls: 12-inch logs will be superior to 7-inch logs in all areas where mass is important.

Fire Safety

Mass also affects fire safety. Heavy logs or timbers are more difficult to kindle or set fire than are smaller framing components such as studs and joists. A log may smolder and blacken or char, but it will not easily support combustion. Architects know that log or timber framing will resist fire damage to a greater extent than will steel beams, because steel subjected to high heat has a tendency to soften and warp, pulling the structure into itself and destroying it.

Mass Effect

Thermally, there is what researchers refer to as the "mass effect." To quote the brochure of the Log Homes Council: "The mass effect relates to the phenomenon in which heat transfer through the walls of a building is delayed by the high heat (retention) capacity of the wall mass. Consequently the demand for heating or cooling energy to maintain indoor temperature may, under some circumstances, be pushed back until a time when wall heat transfer and equipment operating conditions are most favorable. This heat retention phenomenon is also referred to as 'thermal capacitance' or time lag — the resistance of a material (such as solid wood walls) over time, to allow a change of temperature to go from one side to the other."

Everyone is aware that well-built masonry fireplaces use firebricks (mass) to absorb and reflect heat. Heavy masonry walls (called Trombe walls) and concrete floors are built to absorb and hold solar heat. Framed walls, with less mass than masonry or solid wood, simply cannot absorb or store much heat. Framed walls are thus more easily affected by fluctuating temperatures or by wide differences between interior and exterior temperatures.

TECHNICAL DATA OF TEST INFORMATION

The following technical data explains how six test buildings were constructed, and the details of the tests. Refer to the three illustrations, using the identifying numbers assigned to the buildings, to understand how the various types of construction performed.

Test Limitations

The National Bureau of Standards notes that there are limitations to the tests, and that these limitations should be kept in mind when you are considering the test results. For example, there were no interior partitions or furniture in any of the buildings; these materials would provide some mass effect for the wood framed buildings. Also, the windows were closed at all times, and the buildings were designed and constructed so as to maximize the mass effect attributable to the walls. Finally, the study notes that the tests are "very climate dependent," and the results relate to the moderate climate found at the test area of Gaithersburg, Maryland, near Washington, DC.

Description of Test Buildings

All six test buildings were 20 feet wide by 20 feet long; with 7$\frac{1}{2}$-foot high ceilings and no partitions (a single room). Each had four insulating glass (double pane) double-hung windows, with exterior storm windows. Total window area was 11 percent of the floor area. Each building had a single insulated metal door. Each building had a pitched roof and an attic. Attic ventilation was provided using both soffit and gable vents.

Each ceiling had an 11-inch thick (R-34) fiberglass insulation blanket. This uniformity of ceiling insulation in all the buildings ensured that the test results would reflect the thermal performance of the walls only. The edges of the slab-on-grade concrete floors were insulated with 1-inch thick polystyrene insulation at both inner and outer surfaces of the footings. Each building was equipped with a 4.1 KW electric forced air heating plant, and a 13,000 Btu/h split vapor-compression air conditioning system. Again, having the same floor construction and insulation, as well as having identical heating and cooling equipment, helped ensure that any differences noted in thermal performance between the six buildings would reflect on the thermal performances of the wall construction.

Construction Details of Walls

#1: An insulated wood frame home, nominal R-12 (without mass) with $\frac{5}{8}$-inch exterior wood siding, 2 x 4 stud walls, 3$\frac{1}{2}$-inch thick fiberglass insulation, plastic vapor barrier, and $\frac{1}{2}$-inch wallboard.

#2: An uninsulated wood-frame home, nominal R-4 (without mass), same detail as house #1 above, but without fiberglass insulation.

#3: An insulated masonry house, nominal R-14 (with exterior mass), with 4-inch brick, 4-inch block, 2-inch polystyrene insulation, plastic vapor barrier, furring strips, and $\frac{1}{2}$-inch wallboard.

#4: An uninsulated masonry house, nominal R-5 (with exterior mass) with 8-inch concrete block, furring strips, vapor barrier, $\frac{1}{2}$-inch wallboard, and no polystyrene insulation.

#5: A log house, nominal R-10 (with inherent mass) with 7-inch solid square wood logs with tongue-and-groove mating system, no additional insulation, no vapor barrier, and no interior wallboard. (Note: The use of logs of larger diameter — i.e., greater mass — would greatly increase the energy

A – Intermediate Heating

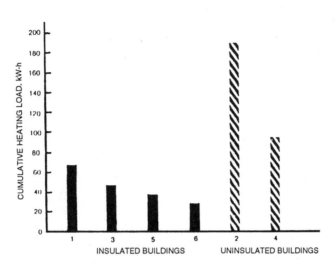

During this 3-week intermediate (spring/fall) heating season, the log building #5 used 46% less heating energy than the insulated wood frame building #1.

B – Summer Cooling

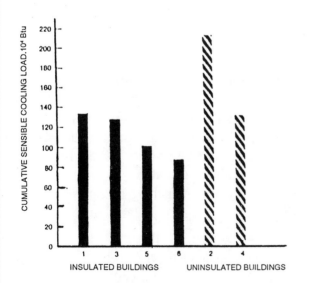

During this 11-week summer cooling season, the log building #5 used 24% less cooling energy than the insulated wood frame building #1.

C – Winter Heating

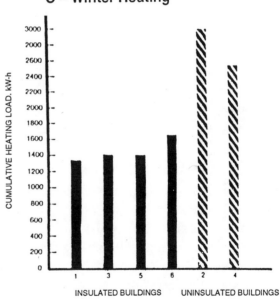

During this 14-week winter heating season, the R-10 rated log building #5 used almost the same amount of heating energy as building #1, the insulated wood frame with its R-12 walls and building #3, the insulated masonry building with its R-14 walls.

and other performance factors of the building. Using logs of 12-inch diameter, rather than the 7-inch diameter used, would have increased the performance gap between the log and the wood-framed buildings.)

#6: An insulated masonry house, nominal R-12 (with interior mass) with 4-inch brick, 3½-inch loose fill perlite insulation, 8-inch concrete block, and ½-inch interior plaster walls.

If you will refer to the three performance Charts A, B, and C, you will see that during a three-week test period when outdoor temperatures were moderate, reflecting weather one would expect to see in the spring or fall heating periods, the log building (#5) used 46 percent less heating energy than was used by the insulated wood-frame building (#1). These results are shown in Chart A. Keep in mind that the log building (#5) was rated as having an R-factor that was 17 percent less than the insulated wood frame building (#1), yet the log wall used 46 percent less heating energy.

In Chart C, we see a fourteen-week-long heating energy comparison, testing during the coldest part of the winter. Here we see that the log building (#5) used approximately the same amount of heating energy as was used by the insulated wood frame building (#1). These results reflect the truth of what we proposed in our discussion of R-factors: the rate of heat loss or flow increases as outside temperatures drop and the temperature differential widens between the inside and outside temperatures.

Chart B compares the amount of cooling energy consumed by the six different buildings during the eleven-week summer cooling season. As Chart B shows, the log building (#5) used 24 percent less cooling energy than was used by the insulated wood-frame building (#1) during the most demanding cooling period. Again, keep in mind that the log building (#5) has an R-factor rating that is 17 percent lower than the R-factor of the insulated and wood-framed building (#1), yet the log building uses 24 percent less cooling energy than is used by the insulated wood-framed building.

The conclusion one may draw from studying these charts is that R-factors are an imprecise way to rate the energy efficiency of a building or a building material, or to compare the potential or in-place performances of various types of construction. The problem lies not with any attempt on the part of builders or manufacturers to deceive the consumer, but in the failure of the entire housing industry, including concerned government agencies, to recognize that R-factors are not static, but that they change with the seasons and circumstances.

CONCLUSION

Our goal in this chapter is to list some basic misconceptions concerning log houses, to dispel myths regarding the energy efficiency of log construction, and to consider the role that mass plays in making a house more comfortable.

The Importance of Building with Mass

As we have discussed, building with mass results in a house that is more comfortable and is less expensive to heat and cool because mass helps to moderate heat loss and thermal cycles. Log houses, having greater mass, are also quieter than stick-built houses, because mass plays a crucial part in controlling sound transfer. Mass also plays a role in making a building more fire resistant, because larger logs do not kindle or burn as rapidly as dimensional lumber does. Logs will burn, of course, but their slowness to kindle ensures precious extra time for the occupants to discover the fire and to take remedial action. And again, if one wishes to increase the mass and performance of the log building, one would only have to use logs of larger diameter than those used in the test.

Finally, building with logs can reduce future decorating and maintenance costs. Unlike plaster or wallboard interiors, which need cleaning, patching, and painting every few years, all-wood log interiors may be sealed when new, and then not need further attention for twenty years or more.

The same may be said for maintaining the exteriors of log houses. Because of the mass or thickness of the logs, and because wood has a tendency to absorb and give up moisture as the humidity and the temperature change, log houses should never be finished with paint or varnish, either of which will leave a film or coating that will crack and peel as the logs expand and contract. Instead, log house exteriors should be treated with a wood preservative, followed by an exterior penetrating finish (stain). Future maintenance should be limited to renewing that penetrating stain as recommended by the manufacturer. (This subject is dealt with in greater detail in Chapter 6.)

3.
Options

I'll have a window seat broad and deep
Where I can sprawl to read and sleep
With windows placed so I can turn
And watch the sunsets blaze and burn ...

As with planning any type of housing, there are a great number of options available for the consideration of buyers of log and timber houses. These options can greatly affect the way a house wears and its livability for your family. Although most of the companies that offer log and timber kit houses provide catalogs of stock plans, the majority of buyers do not simply accept these plans as they are offered. Most of the stock plans bought are customized to fit the individual buyer's needs.

PERSONALIZED DESIGNS

Most manufacturers of log and timber kit houses today offer computer-aided design, known as CAD, which can help you come up with a design that will reflect your family's needs and lifestyle. Roof styles are available in gable, saltbox, chalet, A-frame, dormer, prow, or gambrel designs. L-shaped floor plans may sometimes feature two different roof styles and have one wing roof in A-frame design, with the second wing roof built in a simple gable.

In addition to alterations in such basic areas as foundations, floor space, room size, roof style, and general configuration, you may elect to upgrade window and door choices to obtain better energy efficiency, or you may choose to buy a window(s) on the basis of its size or style if the stock window offerings are too limited. When selecting roofing, you may also choose from almost unlimited shingle or shake styles and colors, including asphalt shingles in wood tones. Some house plan catalogs will show certain models complete with a porch or deck on one or more sides, or may indeed feature a veranda-style porch covered by a roof. Such a porch may extend to all sides of the house.

Garages

Another option the buyer must choose is the garage. Again, many of the house plans featured in catalogs have attached garages. If your particular plan does not, or if you feel that having the attached garage is too contemporary and detracts from the nostalgia and authenticity of the log house, there are dealers who offer plans — or will custom design — for log garages and other outbuildings, too.

The Unique Appeal of Log Homes

The particular point you should keep in mind is this: to a greater extent than most houses, log and timber houses have a certain look and appeal that is unique. The owners of a stick-built house may build the house, live in it for a few seasons, then decide to build additions or outbuildings; however, this approach may not work so easily for the owners of log and timber houses. Whereas the owner of a stick-built home can usually match his building materials at any home center or lumber yard, the owner of the log or timber home must usually go back to the kit manufacturer to obtain materials to match his existing house.

This house has clapboard siding, a wrought iron deck rail, a fireplace, and a sunroom. This fits-anywhere design is a Lindal Cedar Home. Courtesy of Lindal Cedar Homes, Inc.

Avoiding "Afterthoughts"

It has often been noted that the true test of a successful remodeling or addition is that it be done in such a way that the addition appears always to have been part of the original structure, not looking like an "add-on." For most conventional or stick-built houses this can easily be accomplished with good design. But for the log or timber house, any addition to the homestead, whether it be an actual addition to the house structure or a garage or other outbuilding just added onto the land, must be planned to blend in with the house construction to avoid a decided and unwanted contrast or "afterthought" look.

For an example, consider perhaps the most popular of house "add-ons," the porch or deck. Would you want to add a deck built of ordinary dimensional lumber to the side of a conventional round log house? My old partner would protest that you were "putting earrings on a pig"; i.e., the addition does nothing to complement the subject. Our advice: to the extent possible, so far as energy and finances will allow, try to anticipate the finished canvas, and build complete or at least plan ahead to ensure that when your homestead is finished the total effect is one of harmony and balance.

FOUNDATIONS

The foundation of your house may be dictated in part by the type of house you choose to build on it. You should get the advice of your house kit manufacturer or builder before finalizing any plans. In some cases, these all-wood houses can be heavy, and may need special foundations to support them.

Posts or Piers

Most of the kit houses can be built on any conventional type of foundation. If your house is near a flood plain, where high water may occur, you may want to build it atop posts or piers. In hot climates, having the house above ground can aid in cooling and ventilation, as air is allowed to circulate in the space beneath the house. If you travel to Galveston, for example, you will see that the houses on this Texas island are built on posts, a constant reminder of the hurricanes that occasionally sweep the island, bringing flood tides. Many houses that are built atop posts or piers use lattice as a decorative finish to hide the piers. Lattice not only is decorative, but it lets air — or water — circulate underneath the house, and it also provides a barrier to keep out animals.

Conventional Basement

If you are building in a cold climate, and your house is intended for year-round occupancy, you may choose to build over a conventional basement foundation. Having a basement beneath house floors helps to ensure warm floors in cold climates.

Crawlspace

If you are building where the water table may be high but the chances of flooding are slight, or you need a frost footing but do not want a basement, you may choose to build on a crawlspace foundation. Again, the only limit on your choice of foundations is the recommendation of the kit house manufacturer. Do not let your own judgment supersede the judgment of the builder. There are very sound reasons why foundations in a given area tend to follow in similar style. Soil type, water tables, and deep winter frostlines can all affect foundation designs. Make your own foundation choice, within the parameters set down by your builder and by local building codes.

PORCHES AND DECKS

In past decades, the porch was as much a part of the house as the roof, and each house included a porch, at least in front, but usually also in the back of the house. In the post-World War II era, as building lots became smaller and houses became more expensive, porches were sacrificed in the name of space and economy. But there are very good reasons for including a porch in the house plan, and porches have staged a dramatic comeback. Not only is the more traditional porch becoming popular again, but the modern version of the porch — a recreational deck — has proven to be the most popular house addition.

Energy Efficiency

Why should you include a porch or deck in your new house plan? The porch, especially a porch complete with a roof, is a great aid in making your house energy efficient. The porch roof helps shield the house walls from the direct rays of the sun, shading and cooling the house in summer. In winter, this sheltering roof keeps the snow away from the walls and helps minimize the effect of heat loss caused by bitterly cold winds as they move over the house siding.

Protecting Logs

In addition to increased energy efficiency, a roofed porch also helps to protect the walls of log or timber from the drying and bleaching rays of the sun and from the mildew and finish erosion of the rain. To observe the damaging effect of direct sun and rain on paint or stain, check any front door that is partly protected by a storm door. You will find that the area of the front door that is struck by direct sunlight or rain will be much more aged and faded than those portions of the house front door that are shaded by the storm door.

Reducing Cleaning Chores

The addition of a porch or deck will also help to keep your new house clean and reduce house-cleaning chores. Most of the dirt in a house (up to 95 percent, according to professional janitorial companies) is carried or tracked into the house on people's shoes. Walking across a porch or deck before entering the house will knock most of the dirt and grit from your shoes. This is an especially important feature to include if your new log or timber house is sited in the country or along sandy beaches at a lake or an ocean. All these home sites will suffer from a dirt and cleaning problem if you fail to plan properly.

Space for Entertaining

If you have a large family or are fond of entertaining large groups of people, a porch or deck offers low-cost living space. A deck is often preferable to a patio, because the deck, being above ground level, will dry more quickly after a rain, so you don't have to delay the fun until the patio dries. And the same cracks between the deck board that let the rain drip quickly away also let the sand and grit fall from your feet or shoes, reducing the amount of dirt and grit tracked into the house.

Not to neglect what is perhaps the most important feature, a deck or porch provides a perfect place for outdoor recreation and entertaining. You can hang a porch swing or a hammock from the ceiling, take advantage of the shade and outdoor breezes, and have space for al fresco entertaining, so you don't have to cancel the barbecue just because rain threatens. To be sure your deck or porch blends with the house, consider including it in your initial plans, so it can be designed and built by the manufacturer to perfectly complement the house construction.

WINDOWS

Log and timber house construction has come a long way since the frontier homesteader sang, "Oh, the hinges are of leather, and the windows have no glass, and the doors they let the howlin' blizzard in ..." Modern windows combine function, style, low maintenance, and energy efficiency to protect and complement the house.

The Energy Question

Following the days of the oil embargo in the late 1970's, window construction underwent a total redesign. Because windows were seen as a major source of heat loss, energy-conscious designers urged that builders eliminate windows where possible. They especially campaigned against having windows in the north side of the house. Window manufacturers, of course, opposed any reduction in the use of windows, rightly pointing out that the windows saved electricity by providing daylight, and also helped heat the house interior via solar heat gain through the panes.

We should remember here that residential heat loss operates on a "weakest link" principle: heat flows to cold, and it will do so in any direction it can. The

Log houses can be as rustic or as contemporary as you choose. This interior emphasizes the wood look in the ceilings, beams, and deck/balcony railings, with all the cedar accents a gray-tone white; the wallboard is painted light blue. Courtesy of Lindal Cedar Homes, Inc.

best-insulated walls and ceilings you can build will not result in overall heating efficiency if you permit heat loss through another path, such as poor windows or doors. If heat cannot pass through insulated walls, it will simply move through the path of least resistance, so it is necessary to be sure that all the building components you choose are the most energy efficient materials possible.

To resist the movement toward reducing the number of windows used in houses, the window manufacturers redesigned the weatherstripping of the windows to reduce air infiltration, and also developed low-E (low-emissivity) glass and multi-pane windows, and filled the space between window panes with insulating gases rather than dead air. As a result of this research and development in window technology, today's windows are much more energy efficient than even the most expensive windows of a generation ago.

Window Options

Few building components have as great an effect on the appearance or livability of the house as do the windows. Windows are available as bays, bows, double-hungs, sliders, casements, and fixed or thermopane picture windows. And about a decade ago, we saw an industry resurgence in the popularity of the roof window or skylight.

Any or all of these styles may be used in a log or timber home. The double-hung window is perhaps the most energy efficient of the movable or operable windows, and is generally considered superior to the sliders in this area. Bay windows are especially attractive, but are even more so when they overlook a stunning landscape or view and are used in conjunction with a window seat where the family can sprawl to loaf or sleep.

Picture windows became popular in the mass-production housing of the post-World War II era. Today, the picture window has given way to window walls to provide the maximum expression of the phrase, "a room with a view." These window walls are often seen in log or timber houses that are bordered by scenic landscapes such as waterfront, beaches, forests, or mountains.

Roof Windows

There has also been a great increase in the popularity of roof windows for use in log or timber houses. Roof windows can provide needed ventilation, can be used as a natural light source for inside rooms such as bathrooms or halls, and can provide both light and a natural exhaust of kitchen smokes or odors when positioned over the kitchen sink, range, grill, or cabinet worktop. Roof windows also can reduce or eliminate the need for air conditioning. In hot weather, the roof windows on the ceilings and low-level wall windows can be opened during the cool of the evening to provide whole-house ventilation. This system uses the "chimney effect" caused by hot air rising. If you open roof windows when night air is cool, the interior hot air rises and exits through the roof windows. This action creates a suction or draft behind it, pulling cool outside air into the house through the low-level wall windows. During the day, windows are closed to prevent hot outdoor air from being pulled into the house interior, and cooled interior air is retained.

Roof windows can, of course, be used anywhere, and are commonly seen in family rooms or libraries, in foyers, in bathrooms (perhaps over hot tubs), or wherever additional light or ventilation is needed. But perhaps the most popular location for a roof window is over the bed, in a bedroom or loft ceiling. There is an indescribable feeling of peace when you view a starlit night sky — or the northern lights — from the snug comfort of your bed.

Placement of Windows

The log house manufacturer or your builder can advise you on the best placement of windows, and on what type will work best in a given situation. In cold climates, it is accepted environmental wisdom to limit the number of windows with northern exposure, where prevailing winter winds can grab the heat away. In warm climates, window glass with exposure to solar heat gain is viewed as undesirable when considered purely from a point of energy conservation. By the same token, if windows are sheltered and protected from direct sunlight and winter winds by a roofed porch or a wide roof soffit or overhang, energy losses through the windows are limited. Considering the energy efficiency of modern windows, window placement becomes a smaller problem when considering energy conservation.

The bottom line, I think, comes down to a conversation I had some years ago. I went to Wisconsin to inspect a four-season energy-efficient room constructed by Andersen Windows, Incorporated. The room had a concrete floor that served as a collector of solar energy, when winter sun rays penetrated into the room. The room was monitored by computers, to measure heat gain/loss. The premise was that a window room, properly managed, was in fact an energy plus, not an energy loss.

As I toured the house and the new room, I commented to the owner that I thought a couple of the windows violated the "no north" concept, an odd situation in a house that was remodeled to serve as a test room for Andersen Windows. The lady looked at me and replied: "Yes, that is true ... but I wanted windows there, because the view is so pretty." Enough said. No reasonable person will sacrifice the plus of a beautiful view in return for such a minimal energy savings.

DOORS

It used to be thought that only massive plank doors were appropriate for a log or timber house. Or, in a warm climate, one might choose a hand-carved wood door, perhaps one made of oak plank that was not only a door but was also a one-of-a-kind work of art. Today, because of concern with energy efficiency, the buyer of a log or timber home often chooses an insulated metal door, complete with magnetic weatherstripping.

Metal Doors

The metal door no longer has to look like metal. Metal or vinyl doors are available with a grain pattern. Most can be stained to simulate wood, and decorative molding can be applied to break up the flat metal panels. Any door can be wood-grained, using special painting tools, to look like real wood.

These insulated metal doors are about twice as energy efficient as the old wood primary door/

storm door combination, so you don't have to install a combination storm/screen door to keep energy costs low. Of course, if you are living in bug country, where insects are a problem, you will need screen doors if you want to leave primary doors open for ventilation. If insects are not a problem in your area, having the primary door exposed to full view for curb appeal is usually a more authentic look than a door/screen door arrangement. If insects are no problem and you want a wood look, consider installing a Dutch door, a two-piece door that permits you to open the top half for ventilation and view, while leaving the bottom half of the door closed to keep out passing unwanted animal or other guests.

FIREPLACES AND WOOD-BURNING STOVES

Fireplaces and wood-burning stoves are such popular options that we devoted an entire chapter to the subjects, Chapter 7. But because 78 percent of American home buyers name the fireplace as the most sought-after optional feature, a brief review of the most-wanted option bears repeating.

First, more than 55 percent of wood stove purchases and more than 75 percent of fireplace purchases are the result of new construction or remodeling. A buyer's profile of hearth furnishing consumers would parallel the purchasers profile for log or timber homes: median age, thirty-four; median household income, $36,000; 80 percent have attended college; and 94 percent own their own homes.

Wood Stove Designs and Options

Wood stove designs include sleek curves and a rainbow of vivid colors. Some have soapstone, marble, porcelain, or ceramic exteriors in addition to the more familiar cast-iron look. Glass doors replace the old cast-iron doors, so you can enjoy the visible glowing flame, just as with an open fire. You can choose a model that offers one, two, three, or even four-sided views of the fire, and can be used as unique room dividers. Two-sided models can fit into a corner, while the four-sided model can be a centerpiece for a room. The glass door options include

Lindal's sunroom addition brings the outdoors in. The sealing system does not use messy caulks: it's all in the leak-proof fit of the joints. The Straight Eave mullions feature bird's-mouth joints to make a connection that is air- and watertight. Courtesy of Lindal Cedar Homes, Inc.

larger viewing areas (more glass), plus glass that is virtually self-cleaning. These cleaner glass systems employ air-flow systems to "wash" soot and smoke from the glass. One type of glass door employs an infrared barrier that reflects the heat back into the firebox. Heat-shielding systems let one position the wood stove or heater within one foot of a wall without fear of fire.

The many sizes and types of wood heaters will let you select a model that perfectly fits your own heating needs. Wood heaters are made to heat a small room or an entire house: some models have circulating fans to move heated air throughout the room or into adjacent areas.

When designing your log or timber house, choose a wood heater to complement each area where you expect to lounge and rest. You will find the investment to be a wise one, both in terms of financial return and in pure living satisfaction. To quote Anatole France: "The domestic hearth. There only is real happiness."

GARAGES AND OUTBUILDINGS

As you will see in the log and timber home catalogs, the floor plans often incorporate an attached garage. Many people think that in the 1990's, with log and timber homes incorporating contemporary materials and design, an attached garage does not interfere with the aesthetics. But there are some purists who think that attaching a garage to a log or timber house ruins the concept, and these choose to build houses from kits without garages.

If you choose a house kit that does not include an attached garage, check with the manufacturers listed in our Appendix, or with your own house kit source, to find garages or other outbuildings with a log design. Some companies specialize in designing outbuildings that will complement your log home. For example, Amerlink Ltd. shows four different log garage designs in their current catalog. The garages have quality log siding to match your log home. They are available in a number of configurations. Amerlink's Essex model, 24 feet x 24 feet, is a double garage in a gambrel roof design with lots of loft storage space. The Cheshire model, also 24 feet x 24 feet, has a gable roof and could also have loft storage. The Morgan model, 24 feet x 30 feet, has a double garage with a separate space at one end, with its own door, for shop or storage. The Surrey model is 24 feet x 36 feet and has only a single garage door. The rest of the garage space can be used for a shop, a children's play area, storage, or whatever is needed. There is also a lean-to storage shed off the end of the building, where one could store firewood or yard and garden tools. The Surrey model also has a loft space with plenty of headroom, so storage capacity is virtually unlimited.

4.
Choosing the Log or Timber Home

The beams of my house will be fragrant wood ...

After much consideration, you have about convinced yourself that you are ready to build a log or timber house. At the least, you would like to explore the idea further. How can you go about choosing a log or timber home?

THE *LOG HOME GUIDE*

The first step might be to check the newsstands for a copy of *Muir's Original Log Home Guide*. First published in 1978, the guide has been a rallying and unifying force behind the emergence of the log home industry.

The *Log Home Guide*, published quarterly, is chock-full of log home editorial and advertising, both of which can provide further information in your quest for log home guidance. The *Guide* offers an array of back issues, a Log Home Industry Supplier guide, and a Log Builder/Dealer Registry to help put prospective buyers in touch with builders and dealers. The *Guide* also offers an extensive library of books covering all aspects of log home building, as well as several special Log Home Decor issues, which will provide a useful guide to help you furnish and decorate the finished home. The current price is $19.95 for four quarterly issues plus the Annual

Directory of log home companies. You can find the *Log Home Guide* on newsstands, or write to:

Muir Publishing Company, Inc.
164 Middle Creek Road
Cosby, TN 37722-9533
(800) 345-LOGS (U.S.)
(800) 237-2643 (Canada)

Browsing through the *Log Home Guide*, you may spot a dealer whose homes appeal to you. You also will find a complete listing of members of the North American Log Homes Council in our back-of-book Appendix. These dealers offer a wide variety of starter information, including introductory brochures that briefly describe exactly what types of homes each company offers. If one or more of these companies has products that appeal to you, you can send off an order for a plan catalog. Prices of the log home catalogs vary, but these catalogs can get you into the types of home designs offered. Some companies also offer inexpensive videotapes of their operations and products that will help you in making your choice.

PRELIMINARY DESIGN

In a book prepared by the Timberpeg company and titled *Artisan*, architect Stanley F. Nielsen, AIA, offered some great suggestions for designing your next home. A brief outline of Nielsen's recommendations for designing your home begins with the following points:

1. Identify your parameters.
2. Understand your lifestyle.
3. Choose your preferences.
4. Start sketching.

Nielsen goes on to identify the key factors in each of these four points. You might begin this procedure by picking up a yellow legal pad and sharpening your pencils. When you have worked your way through these four points, noting your preferences at each stage, you should have a good preliminary design, and you will be ready to start looking for a manufacturer or builder.

IDENTIFY YOUR PARAMETERS

Budget
Nielsen suggests that your first parameter must be to consider your budget, because your budget will have an effect on almost every one of the hundreds of decisions you must make in the planning stage. From overall size or floor space, to the kind of material you will choose for your floors and kitchen countertops, to the style of light fixtures, every decision will be limited by the amount of money in the budget.

Land
The next parameter Nielsen suggests is to survey the land on which you will build. This includes looking at the contour of the land. Is your building site flat, so it can accept almost any home style, or should you be thinking of a design that will fit a slope or hill? Which way will your house face, and how many windows will be needed to take advantage of the best views? How can you build so that you avoid damaging or removing mature trees, which add value and beauty to your site?

Consider the path of sunlight. In a cold climate, you should position your house to take advantage of solar gain in winter. In a warm climate, you should build roof overhangs or porches to block sunlight, plus siting your house so that solar heat gain is minimized. For example, this may mean positioning your house so that bedrooms are on the east end of the house, away from the heat of a setting summer sun.

Local Building Codes and Restrictions
The final parameters are local building codes and restrictions. Depending on the area, you may have to consider building codes that dictate limits because of such natural factors as earth tremors or quakes, winter snow loads, windstorm dangers, and rising waters on flood plains or shorelines. There may also be exclusionary restrictions regarding the size or style home you can build in a given development. Some zoning restrictions can be very strict, dictating such things as house siding materials and even the exterior colors you may choose. Check with your local building department to get all the facts on any codes or restrictions for your area.

UNDERSTAND YOUR LIFESTYLE

Bedrooms
Nielsen asks: How many primary bedrooms do you need, and how will you use them? Will children share a bedroom, or do circumstances dictate that each child needs a private room? If a bedroom will be for sleeping, it can be quite small; but if a teenager's room also serves as a study, the room must include space for a desk and a computer terminal. Will the master bedroom be a suite, with dressing areas and walk-in closets, or a simple sleeping retreat? Should the master bedroom be upstairs, or in a separate wing for privacy, or near a child's nursery? What are the ages and physical limitations of family members? Do you often have sleep-over guests, and who are they? Can a sofabed in a den serve for infrequent guest sleeping needs, or would you like a guest suite for the comfort of visiting grandparents? Consider all sides of the question carefully before making any decisions.

Kitchen, Bathrooms, and More

Also, consider how you use the kitchen. Are meals unscheduled, eat-on-the-go events, or are you a gourmet cook who loves to stage formal dinners? Do you need room for two cooks, so that each must have his or her own work station? Should the kitchen and dining areas be walled so that they can be closed off for formal affairs or catered meals, or are most parties family affairs that demand a "great room" concept, leaving the kitchen open to the crowd? How many bathrooms will be required to serve your family size and lifestyle, and where will extra baths be located? Would decks and patios adjoining dining or living room help expand the space in your smallish house and open it to large-scale entertaining?

Special Use Spaces

What sort of "special" rooms might you include in your dream house? Do you want a home gym for fitness advocates, a library or home office for at-home business use, or a media room for your listening and viewing pleasure? Now is the time, during the planning stage, to consider your every dream, even though the budget may occasionally bring you back to reality.

The Home as a Whole

Is the home to be the ultimate and final dream home, or a stepping stone home in a fast-track journey? How long will you live in this home? Will your lifestyle change? If you are middle-aged, think about such items as features that promote barrier-free living for the elderly or handicapped. If you are young and your family small, consider choosing a home design that has enclosed space for future expansion, or can be easily added onto if an extra wing is needed later.

CHOOSE YOUR PREFERENCES

For many people, this is the most satisfying stage. Nielsen recommends that you choose colors, textures, sizes, shapes, and arrangements to match your family's tastes. Most experts advise that you study magazines and tear out ideas you like to make a reference file for decorating tips. One novel point that Nielsen makes is to look through design and decorating magazines, and tear out the pages that show any ideas or designs that you either particularly like or don't like.

Nielsen suggests that you save photos of fireplaces, exterior and interior styles, kitchens, built-ins such as shelving, desks, and entertainment centers, and extra features such as skylights or hot tubs. Nielsen points out that a complete file, loaded with ideas you like, will help you bring the entire image of your finished home into sharp focus. By including a file of styles and designs you definitely do *not* like, you will help the manufacturer's design studio zero in on a final plan more quickly.

START SKETCHING

Before getting down to details, you must have an overall plan. Setting down your ideas on graph paper, begin to estimate the overall size of the house, how many rooms it will be, and the size of each room. The graph paper will let you draw the house and room dimensions to scale. A typical scale to use is 1/4 inch to 1 foot; for example, 10 inches equals 40 feet. You can use an architect's scale rule, found in art or drafting supply stores, to do the scale drawing quickly and efficiently. Work with a sharp lead pencil and keep an eraser handy because you will find yourself moving "walls" quite often.

To begin, answer the following questions:

- Will the house be one story or two?
- How many bedrooms will be needed?
- How many bathrooms will be needed?
- Will the house serve the family only, or will you do much entertaining? (This will affect dining room needs, type and size of kitchen, whether a family room is needed, etc.)
- Will the house have hobby rooms or spaces?
- What type and location of doors and windows are best?
- What special features (fireplaces, whirlpool bath, foyer, walk-in closets, pantry) do you want?

- What exterior features (decks, porches, attached garage) will you need?

Sketch each room or wall that will have unusual features. For instance, there may be a china cabinet built into the dining room wall, or a fireplace wall in the family room or master bedroom suite.

You need not have artistic talent to sketch your ideas, nor must the sketches be to exact scale. Your sketches should be done in pencil, so changes can easily be made as you go along. Although exact, to-scale drawings would be very useful, we are not here referring to final plans. Just try to get all your ideas on paper in recognizable form.

Suppose you plan to have a fireplace wall. Will the face of the fireplace extend from corner to corner, across the entire wall, or will you have a window at either/both ends of the fireplace? Rather than having windows, will a part of the fireplace wall be devoted to bookshelves or cabinets that will hold electronic gear? Make full elevation sketches of the walls (detailing the organizing of all wall features from floor to ceiling).

Similar sketches should be made for any wall that has unusual features. This might include built-in cabinetry, shelving, oversized or unusual windows (such as a bay window/window seat arrangement), or a dressing room with special storage.

Does all this sound too difficult? Simple drafting tools such as a ruler or an architect's scale rule, a T-square, and a compass will let you make simple line drawings. Line drawings are almost always easier to use than mere words when trying to convey your ideas to the contractor or draftsperson who will prepare the final plans.

TIME AND MONEY

Before you begin shopping, stop to consider several points. First, amateurs tend to underestimate both the amount of time and the amount of money

If maintained properly, the traditional log home exterior will last for many years with a minimum of care. Courtesy of Gastineau Log Homes, Inc.

needed to build a house. Most neophytes, contemplating a log home kit that includes "all" the building materials, actually are overlooking some serious expenses. These ignored and/or unscheduled expenses can include excavation, foundation, grading, mechanical costs (wiring, heating, plumbing), water well, septic system, lighting fixtures, appliances, etc. In addition, many buyers overestimate their building skills and end up having to spend extra unplanned funds to have roof framing, roofing, foundation, and other work done by professionals. Most experts estimate that you should start with the price for a complete home kit (more about complete kits later) and double or even triple it to arrive at a more realistic total target price for the completed house.

Pricing

For example, Timberpeg, a major manufacturer of timber (post and beam) homes, supplies a price list that first lists a Package Price Range for each model offered, followed by an Estimated Completed House Cost. For their Mediterranean model 4000 (Timberpeg's model number reflects the approximate finished square footage of the house) the Package Price range is $136,000 to $152,000, while the Completed House cost estimate is between $400,000 and $475,000, or triple the basic Package Price. Or consider that a more modest Carefree Fairway 1000 model has a listed Package Price of $35,000 to $37,000, with a Completed House Cost of $70,000 to $85,000. The completed house price, in addition to the extras already listed, may include transportation, local taxes, decks, patios, and garages. Don't be an optimist when projecting do-it-yourself financial savings, especially if you have no building skills or experience.

Time

Many experts suggest that you should have at least six months of free time available if you expect to do much building yourself. One buyer we read of, who had a considerable amount of construction experience, planned to start a home in April and occupy it in the fall. By winter he had only closed in the exterior. It was a full year and a half before he had

the home completely finished, and even then he had hired substantial parts of the work done.

It is little wonder, then, that companies such as Gastineau Log Homes, Inc., report that a full three-fourths of their homes are constructed by professional builders. Of these, buyers are split between those who have the builder construct a shell home, with the interior to be finished by the buyer, and those who buy the house turn-key or completely finished by the pros. Keep in mind, then, that the key to a happy home-building experience is to study and plan your project carefully. Then revise your time and money estimates upwards by at least 10 percent. Wear your bifocals, not your rose-colored glasses, when estimating both the final cost and the construction time for the house.

A HELPFUL VIDEO

One other aid to exploring the byways of the log home business may be a video program titled *Log Knowledge*. This forty-minute video subtitles itself a "Comprehensive Guide Through the Log Home Industry," with chapters including such subjects as Picking the Right Company, Company Bids, Log Profiles, Horizontal Surfaces, Sealing Systems, Corner Styles, Pre-cut vs. Rough Cut, Financing, Log Grading, North American Log Homes Council, Manufactured vs. Handcrafted, and Green Logs vs. Dry Logs. The video was produced by Brad Burgat, who has been a log home builder. The cost of the video is $29.95. Burgat's company, Buyer Information Services, can be reached at P.O. Box 1025, LaPorte, CO 80535. You can call to order toll-free at (800) 348-9910. The video carries a money-back guarantee of a full refund with no questions asked.

KITS — THREE CHOICES

There are three basic types of log home kits available.

Conventional Style

The first is a conventional log building style, in which actual logs are milled to uniform shape and diameters. The pre-cut kits are available with all materials to complete the house, or the buyer can buy the basic four-wall log shell, then buy other materials locally.

The logs may be from 5 inches to 14 inches in diameter. The logs are stripped of bark, turned so they are uniform in diameter, notched at the ends (corners), with tongue and grooves cut into the top and bottom edges. The logs for exterior walls are fitted together like Lincoln Logs. Gasket and sealant materials are used to ensure that joints are weather-tight. Interior walls are usually conventionally framed, and covered with wallboard or paneling.

This kit, in which the log shell offers a traditional log home look and ease of erection, usually is topped with standard roof trusses, but can have a log roof as well. The full-log construction means there will be considerable shrinking in the exterior walls as the logs dry and season. When wet (uncured) logs are used, this shrinkage can mean a log wall that is built to be 8 feet high may shrink by as much as 6 inches, down to a height of 7 feet and 6 inches, when the log walls season or settle. This shrinkage can play havoc with logs and door and window frames. Interior partitions built to the original log height of 8 feet will not settle as the logs do. The results of this uneven shrinkage can be imagined. The builder must be aware of this future shrinkage and build so as to compensate for it, or logs can twist and check badly as they settle.

Shaped Log Style

The second log home style consists of logs that have been shaped so that they are rectangular or square, rather than left round. The logs may be from 3 inches to as much as 12 inches thick. The log configuration may result in a shiplap siding design on the house exterior, and flat wood walls on the interior. These logs also have gaskets and sealants for the joints, to weatherproof them, and are nailed or screwed together, much as round logs are assembled. The flat wood interior walls make framing for interior partitions much easier to fit, compared to round logs.

Conventional Framing with Half-Round Logs

A third log kit consists of conventionally framed exterior walls, with studs, top and bottom plates, and insulation in the stud cavities. This conventional framing is covered by half-round logs on the exterior, and sometimes on the interior, to maximize the log home effect. This can result in a very warm house, but building time and cost are often increased because the builder is actually building double walls — one a conventionally framed wall and the second, a log wall.

THE LOG HOME KIT — HOW COMPLETE?

When you get down to comparing kit prices, you must be sure that you are comparing apples to apples. If you buy a basic log home kit, which consists only of the log components of your house, you will have a lengthy and costly list of materials to buy at the local lumber yard. Look beyond the base prices of the home kits and check off the materials lists to be sure the kits are complete and comparable.

For example, Log Cabin Homes Ltd. of Rocky Mount, North Carolina lists their kit packages to include:

- Pressure-treated mud sill plate
- 8-inch Log Cabin logs for exterior walls (your choice of white pine, cypress, or western red cedar, double-milled tongue and groove, choose from eight log profiles)
- Two-story homes have full logs for the second story
- One and one-half- and two-story models have second floor joist system
- Double row polyfoam gaskets and siliconized acrylic sealant
- Log spiral spikes needed per plan (optional lag screws)
- Oak joint dowels for all joints and corners
- Window buck frames
- Door buck frames

The dramatic ceiling and wall treatment here highlights the beauty of natural wood.
Courtesy of Lindal Cedar Homes, Inc.

- Window exterior casings
- Door exterior casings
- Owens Corning Fiberglas Premium Windows double-hung insulated low-E glass or Andersen brand alternate
- Trapezoid glass as illustrated
- Exterior doors, weatherstripped by Morgan
- Exterior door locksets
- Total roof system:
    Stress engineered roof rafters
    5/8-inch CDX plywood roof decking
    Asphalt impregnated felt paper
    Fascia with sub-fascia
    Drip edge
    Gable end louvers
    Twenty-year class A fiberglass shingles
- 8-inch Log Cabin gable end siding
- Porch roof system (when illustrated or requested)
    6-inch porch posts
    Carry beams
    Roofing materials
- 2 x 4 interior studding (2 x 6 for plumbing walls)
- Log-i-cal precision engineered blueprints by AutoCAD Systems
- Standard detail sheet (shows standard corner systems and rough openings)
- Log Cabin Homes "How-to" construction guide

This list demonstrates how comprehensive this particular company's kit materials list is. Let us point out that you may have access to standard building materials (everything but the logs) or feel you can buy them at discount locally. Our intent is not necessarily to convince you to buy a complete kit; we only wish to point out that you should consider *exactly* what you will be getting before you make your final buying decision. Be sure that cost comparisons between manufacturers fully recognize any difference in the materials lists.

Log Species

There are further price differences between the wood species offered by the various manufacturers. In the materials list above, Log Cabin Homes Ltd.

gives the buyer a choice between white pine, cypress, and western red cedar logs. Gastineau Log Homes, Inc. offers oak logs; others may offer naturally rot-resistant cypress, redwood, and cedar. Other wood species available include lodgepole pine, northern white cedar, eastern white pine, Douglas fir, and Engelmann spruce.

Custom Design

Log home catalogs are wish-books, but the reality is that very few of the kit homes are sold without design input from the buyer. Computer-aided design (CAD) is a marvelous development that lets you move components around until you get your own particular dream home design. Keep in mind, though, that changes do cost money. Listed home prices go out the window when you get creative with features such as roof windows, stone fireplaces, pegged or parquet custom flooring, handcrafted lighting fixtures, and upscale appliances. Fancy hot tubs will put a decided kink in your plumbing budget. Soaring and beamed cathedral ceilings provide a feeling of spaciousness while subtracting significant amounts from your checkbook.

On the other hand, do not try to start with a basic design and then price out the most expensive alternatives. Try to present to your builder an honest and complete picture of your dream home, including size, number of bedrooms and baths, ceiling and roof construction. At the same time, present your budget goals, and state where you feel you will reach the outer limits of affordability. As planning proceeds, with budget limits in mind, the planner or builder can suggest the compromises you must make to approach your dream home without scuttling your budget.

Controlling Costs

One way to control initial housing costs is to spend your money on those things that are a permanent part of the house and would be difficult to change at a later date. Quality materials and appliances, energy-efficient insulation packages and windows, the hot tub you just can't live without — these

This beautiful staircase is a focal point for the design of this home.
Courtesy of Appalachian Log Homes.

things should be included with the original planning and construction, when installation is easiest.

Keep in mind, however, that you can always install low-budget lighting fixtures, and replace them with custom-made fixtures as the budget permits, to get just that special effect you want. You can cover the floors with low-budget vinyl floor covering, then install that fancy pegged ranch plank flooring or plush carpeting when the budget eases. You can leave some space unfinished. The basement recreation room or loft guest room can be next year's project. You can pour the footings only for that massive stone fireplace and call the mason when the budget can handle it. You can rough in the plumbing for extra bathrooms and install the fixtures later. Garages can be built or added on at a future date, if the budget dictates. Of course, if money is no object, you can do your project up exactly as you wish from beginning to end.

SELECTING THE RIGHT COMPANY

Although there are dozens or even hundreds of builders who hand-craft log homes on a local basis, something like 85 percent of all log homes are built by members of the North American Log Homes Council. Ask the kit company for the name of a builder he works with in your area. Try to visit former customers, and query them to see how satisfied they are. Visit a log home in progress to see firsthand just how much care the builder exercises when building the home. You may even want to plan a vacation so that you can visit the log home company at their home office, so you can see their procedures firsthand. When you sign that contract, you are committing yourself to a long-term relationship. Know as much as you possibly can about the people with whom you will be dealing. Insist on checking out credentials. In addition to membership in the North American Log Homes Council, the log home company may be a member of the Building Systems Council of the National Association of Home Builders, or of regional organizations such as the Southeastern Lumber Manufacturer's Association (SLMA) or the Better Business Bureau. Dealing with members of such organizations may entitle you to access to a review board if any disputes develop. At the very least, being a member of such organizations shows the company is interested in furthering the image of its industry.

5.
Building the Log or Timber Home

The roof must have a rakish dip
To shadowy eaves where the rain can drip
In a damp, persistent tuneful way;
It's a cheerful sound on a gloomy day.
And I want a shingle loose somewhere
To wail like a banshee in despair
When the wind is high and the storm-gods race
And I am snug by my fireplace.

Kits of pre-cut logs or post and beam timbers were once thought of as the ultimate in do-it-yourself building projects. Today, in an era of increased building technology, most manufacturers of log and timber house kits prefer to have their products erected by experienced builders and are not enthusiastic about having their houses assembled by complete amateurs. A house that is not assembled correctly will fail in service and will be a long-standing example of negative advertising, so the manufacturers of these home kits have a vested interest in having their houses properly erected.

SHOULD YOU BUILD YOUR OWN OR HIRE A BUILDER?

It is true that the engineered kits of today are a vast improvement over the log houses offered in the past. No longer does the builder have to sort through a pile of logs, trying to find one more log that matches, as close as nature will allow, with the last log he installed. Most log and timber house kits have components that are pre-cut and shaped so that they fit together with great precision. Still, most manufacturers do not advise that you build your own log or timber home, for a variety of reasons that we will discuss.

Before deciding whether you will build your own log or timber house or hire a contractor, consider these facts.

Time
First, building any house is a major undertaking. Building a house almost always takes more time than we first plan, and the do-it-yourself monetary savings are usually far less than we have anticipated. If you are not an experienced builder (and few of us can claim much experience in building with logs and timbers), the odds are that as you proceed with construction, you will repeatedly encounter problems that will have you stumped. Remember, any time you have to take something apart or pull a nail, you are trying to correct a mistake, and mistakes waste time.

Size
Next, consider the size of your project. A basic two-room log cabin in the woods is one thing; building

Log Style Profiles

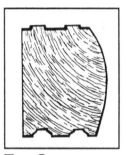

The Original Classic Log

Offers a traditional rounded exterior and a flat interior with the look of V-notched paneling.

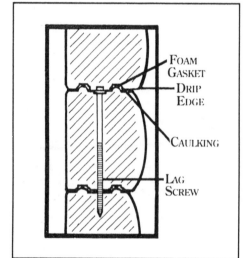

FOAM GASKET

DRIP EDGE

CAULKING

LAG SCREW

The Double-Four Bevel Log

Offers the exterior appearance of New England clapboard siding and a flat interior wall with the look of V-notched paneling.

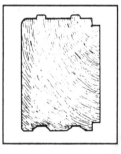

The Chinked Log

Our newest style offers the rustic look of handhewn timers with a "chinking" inlay.

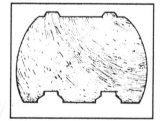

The Double-Round Classic Log

Offers traditional rounded appearance both inside and out. (Frostline only)

The Contemporary Bevel Log

Offers the exterior appearance of clapboard siding and a flat interior wall with the look of V-notched paneling.

Log style profiles.
Courtesy of Amerlink.

your own 5,600-square-foot, two-story ranch home, as one buyer did, is an entirely different matter. This buyer, a sort of jack-of-all-trades who certainly was not an amateur, spent eleven full months building his home — seven months building the home, and four more months building a massive masonry fireplace. Will your budget and career permit you to take that much time from your job? Trying to do two jobs at once, which is basically what you are doing if you are holding down a full-time job and building a house at the same time, will often become first frustrating and then overwhelming, even impossible.

Foundation

What sort of foundation will the house have? These houses can be built over concrete slabs, crawlspace foundations, or full basements. If the house is to be built near a flood plain or beach, in a hot climate, or on a site with distant views, you may decide to build the house above the ground, on piers. Building over some of these foundation choices would be a difficult project that could challenge many experienced contractors, much less an amateur.

Style

Next, consider the style of the house you plan to build. One novice log home builder likened the erection of the tongue-and-groove wall logs to being like "playing with Legos when I was a kid." We have already mentioned that these "Legos" weigh several hundred pounds each. That aside, what happens when you raise the walls to their 8-foot height, and the easy work is done? Will you just set prefab trusses in place and install a wallboard ceiling? Or will your house have cathedral ceilings and/or beams? Will there be a second story or a loft? Will the roof shape be shed, gambrel, saltbox, dormered, and/or gabled? Could you build a roof with these configurations?

Log Considerations

Logs used in house construction can shrink, twist, and split if they are unseasoned or contain more than 20 percent moisture. Some log builders estimate that a wall built of green or wet logs, that is built to be 8 feet high today, may shrink as much as 6 inches and settle down to a wall height of only 7½ feet within a year of construction. This can play havoc with interior wall partitions and door and window frames as the logs shrink away from them. Experienced log builders know how to build to compensate and allow for this shrinkage. Of course, logs that are well seasoned and have a moisture content of 20 percent or less will not experience as much shrinkage. The species of wood that you choose — oak, pine, or whatever — also affects the number of problems you will have as the house seasons and settles. Some wood species tend to twist, warp, and crack more than others. All these factors, and others, should be considered before you decide to tackle the job of building your log or timber home yourself.

HOW LOG HOUSES ARE ASSEMBLED

Long ago, logs for homes were just trees with limbs and bark removed, and the logs had their natural taper: thicker at the butt end, progressively smaller in diameter as you move to the top of the tree. If one stacked the logs so all the thicker butt ends of the logs were on the same end of the wall, and the tapered top ends of the logs at the other, the builder could not maintain a level wall. When building those log homes, the logs were positioned so that the butt end of the tree and the tapered or top end of the log were erected so the ends alternated, and the builder could maintain some semblance of level as the wall went up by choosing and matching his logs carefully.

Joining Methods

The new generation of log houses does not utilize logs that are simply peeled or de-barked trees. The configuration and joining methods for assembling the many kit homes available vary from one manufacturer to another. Each company has its own joining method, usually somewhat like that of other kits available, but most with some variations in design and assembly. The information that follows is general and does not pertain to all the log kit homes available. It is intended only to inform the reader regarding the basic way that log houses go together. For specific information about any particular kit home, consult one of the manufacturers listed in the Appendices.

Today, logs are turned on a lathe so that they are of uniform diameter, from end to end and from log to log. Two sides of the log are then grooved so that the edges of the logs interlock as they are put in place. The matching grooves may be a Swedish cope — sometimes called a saddle notch — a sort of U-shaped groove that lets a log sit atop the log beneath it like a saddle on a horse. Or, more commonly, the top and bottom edges of the log are milled so that they fit tightly together via tongue-and-groove joints. These tongue-and-groove joints not only ensure that the assembled wall will be strong, but that the tightly fitted joints will prevent water entry or air infiltration. Where the logs meet at the corners of the house, the logs may be cut to fit together in a dovetail pattern. This type of corner construction results in a joint that is extremely strong, resulting in a very sturdy building.

Some manufacturers, such as Precision Craft Log Structures, use a double tongue-and-groove on the log edges, and even cut a double tongue-and-groove in the saddle notch at the corners of the logs. They then apply a foam sealant to the tongues, to seal the joint against water and air entry. Rather than using nails or screws to join the logs, as most manufacturers do, Precision Craft ties their logs together using through bolts.

Gaskets, Caulking, and Chinking

As logs are raised, an insulating gasket is placed at each joint. The log edges along the gaskets are coated with a durable caulk, most commonly a silicone caulk product. Ten-inch long galvanized nails or screws are driven to lock the pair of logs together. In some types of log construction, there may be grooves on the inside/outside of the log joints that are designed to be filled with foam insulation and chinking. The chinking serves as both a decorative effect and a barrier to air or water infiltration.

Raising and Placing Logs

Just the sheer weight and bulk of logs and timbers was once a barrier to amateur construction efforts. On the frontier, or where any green logs were used, the weight of the logs could be excessive, far more than one or two workers could handle. The practice once was to lean several logs at an angle, one end of the logs on the ground and the opposite ends atop the partially-erected log wall, to form crude but workable ramps. The next log to be raised was then positioned parallel to the wall, at the base of the ramp logs, and ropes were tied with one end to the log, the other rope end tied to a horse's harness or singletree. By driving the horse forward, the wall log was skidded up the ramp and set in position atop the log wall.

Today, heavy logs and timbers are still lifted into position with machinery, using either a front-end loader mounted on a tractor or a crane to lift the heavy beams or trusses into place. But for many or most log kits, the logs are dried to a moisture content of 20 percent, so that the excess weight of the water is eliminated. The drier logs or timbers are lighter than green logs, and can often be raised into place by two or more husky workers. Still, the length and bulk of the logs and timbers make using manual labor to erect these homes a questionable proposition for many buyers, especially those who do not have a crew of friends and/or relatives to call on when help is needed. It is no mystery why frontier movies, when depicting a barn or cabin raising, showed an entire church congregation, often the entire population of the town, showing up to get the job done. Log construction is not a job for the Lone Ranger: you *will* need help.

ROOFS

The foregoing information is a general description of how the logs in the log homes are assembled, but log homes are not built entirely of logs. After the log

This cutaway illustration from Amerlink shows how their log houses go together.
Courtesy of Amerlink.

Erecting the log walls of an Appalachian Log Home model. Note the crane in background at left: these logs are heavy. Courtesy of Appalachian Log Homes.

Logs for the kit are numbered to guide the builder in assembly. The spaces between the logs are filled with insulation, sealed, and caulked. Courtesy of Appalachian Log Homes.

Roof rafter beams are set atop the log walls. Note the temporary bracing used to hold logs and beams in place until they are secured. Steel scaffold has been erected on the floor to reach the rafters. Courtesy of Appalachian Log Homes.

Rafter beams are tied together using cross-ties called collar beams. Worker fastens the framing together with bolts. Courtesy of Appalachian Log Homes.

Here the front gable is tied into the main ridge beam. Steel scaffold is visible inside, seen between the beams. Courtesy of Appalachian Log Homes.

Another view of the joining of opposing roof gables. Note that with Appalachian Log Homes, the base logs are laid directly on the concrete basement walls, not atop the floor joists/subfloor assembly. This is done to support the weight of the logs. Courtesy of Appalachian Log Homes.

walls are raised, there is the roof structure to consider.

Structure

The roof structure on a log home may be simple carpenter's work. If the house is built in the familiar rectangular shape, the easiest way to build a roof is to set simple pre-stressed roof trusses in place atop the long walls. This type of roof construction results in the conventional roof, with end gables on the house. These end gables can be filled in with logs or can be covered with half-log siding to maintain the log effect all the way up to the roof line.

Shingles

These conventional roofs can be sheathed with plywood and then shingled with asphalt shingles. Asphalt shingles are available in wood tones, and can be had with thick edges that provide a so-called "shadow line" to simulate more expensive wood shingles or hand-split shakes. This type of asphalt shingle roof is quite attractive and may carry a warranty of twenty-five years or more, depending on the manufacturer and the weight of the shingle.

It is true that hand-split cedar shakes are very attractive, but asphalt shingles may be preferred if your house is built in the deep woods or any site where there is high humidity. Because moisture encourages such problems as wood rot, mildew, moss, and mold, constant high humidity conditions are not a good environment for wood shakes. Be aware, however, that wood shakes can be pressure treated to resist insect infestation and decay, and to make them fire resistant. If wood shakes or shingles are your choice for roofing, check with the dealer to help decide what chemical treatments might be advisable for your particular location.

HOW TIMBER HOUSES ARE ASSEMBLED

The first carpenters to reach American shores were ship's carpenters. These ship's carpenters were very necessary crew members in the days of wooden ships and iron men. The ship's carpenter, who in

sailing movies was always nicknamed "Chips," could repair a broken spar, splice or repair broken masts, or patch a damaged plank in the ship's hull.

Those wooden ships had a basic framework made of strong timbers, usually made of dense wood such as oak. The timbers were joined together with mortise-and-tenon joints. In this system of joinery, a slot or mortise is chiseled into a beam at the point where a joint is wanted. Then the end of a post is chiseled to make a tenon or tongue to fit into the mortise. To have maximum strength, the tenon or tongue must fit very tightly into the mortise or slot. A tenon (tongue) that makes a sloppy or loose fit in the mortise (slot) yields a very weak joint that will soon fail. So having a carpenter who was a competent joiner was necessary to build ships that could survive the stresses of ocean storms.

After fitting the tenon into the mortise, a brace, or hand drill, was used to drill a hole through both mortise and tenon. Then a tightly fitted wooden peg was driven through mortise and tenon to lock them into a very strong joint that would not fail when under stress. When the framework or timbers of the ship was joined, thick oak planking was attached with wooden pegs to the timbers of the ship frame.

Historical Uses

This post and beam or timber construction was used to build early houses and commercial buildings in the original colonies along the eastern seaboard of America. Many of the most beautiful and durable of the early homes and buildings employed the post and beam technique of building. Because post and beam construction permitted the use of strong timbers that could span wide spaces and needed no interior load-bearing support walls, larger buildings such as barns were of post and beam construction. This technique of building was the basic approach used on barns, even after the Industrial Revolution produced sawmills and brought us a plentiful supply of cut, or dimensional, lumber. Post and beam construction was still used on barns well into this century. Even today, a short drive into any rural area of America will let you see firsthand just how durable and beautiful these structures can be.

Roof gables, another view.
Courtesy of Appalachian Log Homes.

In later years, beginning in the 1950's, the development of prefabricated roof trusses permitted enclosing of large open areas without interior support walls, and the timbers used in post and beam construction could be replaced by roof trusses of almost any length or span.

If having a roof that will span over wide spaces without having interior load-bearing walls is your only goal, roof trusses will let you accomplish that goal. But wood is the most beautiful, economical, and easy-to-work building material available to man. The warmth of wood, the attractive geometric pattern of the framework, and the artistry and handicraft of the pegged mortise and tenon joints has an appeal that is timeless. Post and beam or timber houses have steadily grown in popularity since the 1970's, a trend that we expect will continue through the foreseeable future. There will be timber houses as long as there is timber.

Tree Species

Today, scientific research has shown that tree species other than oak can be used successfully in post and beam construction. Indeed, in some respects other woods are not only equal, but are in some ways superior, to oak. For example, Timberpeg, The Artisans of Post and Beam, has conducted tests of various wood species. To quote the company's chief executive, Richard Neroni, "But for the most consistent combination of aesthetic beauty and structural stability, we frame primarily with eastern white pine and Douglas fir.

"We've chosen eastern white pine for its unsurpassed aesthetic flexibility. You can leave it untreated, or apply oil, stain, or paint — and it will always look good. It has a straight, subdued grain and a beautifully light, natural color; if left untreated, it will deepen with age to a rich, mellow brown. Our engineers like its stability: compared to most other woods used for timber framing it has less tendency to twist, check, and shrink."

Neroni continues: "When we use Douglas fir, we use exclusively the 'select structural' and 'dense select structural' grades. The primary advantage of Douglas fir is strength — it's superb for spanning long distances; and these export grades, with their tight, straight, relatively knot-free grain, are less likely than others to twist, check, or shrink. Douglas fir has a rich color, and frames cut from Douglas fir are usually more contemporary looking than those cut from eastern white pine."

Why does Timberpeg continue to join their timbers with mortise-and-tenon joints and wooden pegs, long after other manufacturers have begun to use steel plates and bolts? Some people like the appearance of the massive bolts and nuts holding the steel joining plates, but Timberpeg likes the "lasting elegance of our joinery."

Building Techniques
So now that we understand the history of post and beam construction, how are these timber homes built? A framework of horizontal timbers (beams) and vertical timbers (posts) is joined together using mortise-and-tenon joints, secured with wooden pegs that are both structural and decorative (or, in the case of some manufacturers, with steel plates and bolts). These posts and beams are joined to form a complete structural framework. This timber framework provides a building with tremendous strength to resist the stresses of winter snow loads plus the wind load of storms that attack it. The timber framework is exposed on the interior of the building, providing a pleasing geometric design and the massive beam effect. However, if a more contemporary interior is desired, or one wishes to minimize or downplay the effect of the beams, this can easily be done by covering the interior with wallboard or paneling.

The posts and beams support the entire structure, so no interior load-bearing partitions are needed to support the upper floors or to hold up the roof. This means that the interiors of post and beam houses

allow total design flexibility: one can either leave the interior as open, flowing space, or partitions can be built as desired to divide the space into smaller rooms. The choice is yours.

Exterior Shell and Energy Benefits
When the post and beam framework is finished, the exterior shell of the building is erected around the frame. The buyer should be aware that a properly constructed post and beam house will be more energy efficient that a conventional stick-built house. With post and beam construction, the framing supports the exterior shell of the house, but does not interrupt the shell as ordinary platform framing (2 x 4 or 2 x 6 stud walls) does. This means that with stick framing, the insulation barrier is interrupted every 16 or 24 inches, depending on the on-center spacing of the wall studs (16 inches o.c. or 24 inches o.c.). This allows outside air to infiltrate the house and allows heat to be lost at each stud location. It is estimated that up to one-third of the heating energy consumed in a conventional stick-built house may be due to this air infiltration and heat lost through stud interruption of the outer shell.

In addition, with stick-built housing, the fiberglass insulation batts in sidewalls can become wet from transient moisture that passes through the wall into the stud cavity. Being wet can cost fiberglass insulation as much as 50 percent of its efficiency or R-value. Compressing fiberglass batts so they fit behind plumbing, wiring, or framing members also reduces the insulation value of the batts. Other insulation interruptions in stick-built houses occur at the corners where outside walls meet, in the short studs over doors, over and under windows, and at the point or apex of the corner where wall insulation and ceiling insulation are interrupted by the double top 2 x 4 plate.

By contrast, the post and beam house does not use fiberglass batt insulation, so there is no heat loss due to moisture penetration or compressed insulation batts. Instead, post and beam houses use rigid foam insulation panels that are uninterrupted by framing and provide an unbroken envelope so the houses are wrapped in a virtually continuous blanket of insulation. By combining this continuous wall/ceiling insulation barrier with high performance insulating windows and doors, post and beam houses can offer significantly higher energy efficiency than ordinary houses.

Exterior Walls

To build the exterior walls, 1 x 8 tongue-and-groove pine sheathing is first nailed over the post and beam framing. A 6-mil polyethylene vapor barrier is applied directly over the 1 x 8 sheathing. The vapor barrier should be applied so it is continuous, and the polyethylene should be overlapped at any seams or joints in the barrier. Then a layer of polyisocyanurate foam insulation board is applied over the vapor barrier. Over the foam insulation, 1 x 4 strapping boards are nailed to provide support for the siding to come. A layer of Tyvek (an air barrier that prevents outside air from infiltrating the interior of the house, but permits moisture to pass through so it won't be trapped in the wall) is applied. Then the siding, usually ½ x 6-inch cedar clapboards (but some optional siding if desired by the buyer) is nailed onto the 1 x 4 strapping. Cedar trim boards at windows, doors, and soffits complete the exterior wall construction.

Interior

On the interior, the buyer can opt for a look that is predominantly or totally wood, but many buyers choose to use plaster between the beams on some of the walls and/or ceilings. The bare plaster can be left unpainted to get a stark white effect that contrasts with the wood tones of the beams, it can be smoothed for painting in any color, or wall covering can be hung where desired to provide a more eclectic look. Or you can choose any one of a number of textured plaster finishes, ranging from a light stipple or sand float finish to a heavy troweled Mediterranean or Spanish stucco. Emphasizing the contrast and shadows between the massive textures and the wood beams can be a unique and most effective decorating technique, and will help to avoid the cookie-cutter sameness so common in other homes.

Roof

For the roof, 1 x 8 tongue-and-groove pine boards are used for sheathing, exactly like the sidewall construction. Then the 6-mil poly vapor barrier and the polyisocyanurate foam insulation board are applied atop the 1 x 8 pine sheathing. Shake or shingle ribs, 1 x 4's like the sidewall strapping boards, are installed over the insulation board to provide nailers for the cedar shakes or shingles to come. A layer of 30-pound felt paper underlayment is placed between the layers of cedar shakes. A 1 x 8 cedar ridge cap completes the roof construction.

HIRING A CONTRACTOR

Site

You should select your dream building site before deciding on the house plan for you. The way the site or lot lies, whether it is sloped or flat, what and where the interesting views are, your proximity to water or a flood plain — all will affect the house plan you select.

Foundation

When working with the manufacturer's design team to plan your house, you must decide on the type of foundation you will have. You may choose to have a full basement, a crawlspace foundation, a walkout basement level to fit your sloped lot, or you may build your dream house on piers. All these decisions must be made and the foundation built before your home kit is delivered to the site. Failure to have the site properly prepared will only cause expensive delays when the delivery truck can't unload the kit materials.

Erecting the House

How you will choose a contractor and crew to erect your house depends to some extent on which manufacturer you buy the kit from. Some kit manufacturers will not sell their product to a do-it-yourselfer, insisting that they supply their own erection crews. Some have crews who travel with the kit delivery truck, and do the unloading and erection at your site. Others have local or regional representatives who

1. Conventional framing at first floor (supplied by others).
2. Timberpeg pre-cut mortise and tenon frame with 2"x 8" pine decking.
3. 1"x 8" tongue and groove pine.
4. 6-mil polyetheylene vapor barrier (supplied by others) applied directly over 1"x 8".
5. Polyisocyanurate foam insulation board.
6. 1"x 4" strapping.
7. 1/2"x 6" cedar clapboards.
8. Cedar trim.
9. 1"x 4" shake or shingle ribs.
10. 30-pound felt interlayment (supplied by others) between cedar shake layers.
11. Western red cedar shakes or shingles.
12. 1"x 8" cedar ridge cap.
13. Tyvek (or equal) air barrier (supplied by others).
14. Andersen™ Perma-Shield® Low E windows -- style per plan.

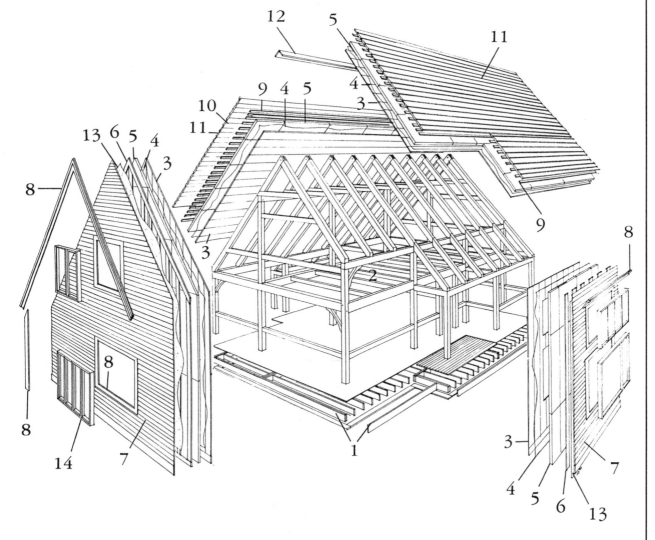

This illustration shows the construction of a Timberpeg timber home. The framework of timbers provides the strength and support, the exterior sheathing, insulation, and siding are applied over the framework as an envelope. No interior support walls are needed; timber homes offer the ultimate in interior flexibility. Courtesy of Timberpeg.

will actually do the erection work or will supervise the crew you choose.

Timberpeg, for example, will not actually erect your house kit, but will connect you with a local Timberpeg Independent Representative. The representative will provide full planning and design help, and will coordinate the complete manufacturing and delivery process. He or she will also work with your contractor to help oversee the erection of the kit, and will assist in getting a bid from your contractor so you can determine the final cost of your house.

6.
Finishing and Maintaining the Wood Home

... Then when my house is all complete
I'll stretch me out on the window seat
With a favorite book and a cigarette
And a long cool drink that my cook will get
And I'll look about my bachelor nest
While the sun goes streaming down the west ...

When buying or building a new house, many of us are thinking only about affordability, so we consider only the initial price. Actually, we should broaden that view and understand that there are at least two factors involved in the expense question to consider when buying or building a new house.

EXPENSE FACTORS

The House Itself
The first factor is the primary cost of the house itself: building materials, labor, permits, and land. These expenses are difficult for the consumer to control, because land prices, material prices, and labor costs are set by the local marketplace. Our goal then should be not just to buy the least expensive house, but to get our money's worth, to make a housing investment that will appreciate over the years.

Future Maintenance
But there is a second expense factor to consider when building or buying a house, one that we often or usually ignore, and that is the cost of living in that house, or the total cost of future maintenance. By choosing quality building materials, appliances, and furnishings, the consumer can have a great effect on the yearly cost of future maintenance. While the unwary buyer may buy a house on the basis of initial cost alone, businesses, as well as savvy consumers, buy not on initial cost alone, but on the basis of life cycle costing. Life cycle costing considers not only initial cost, but initial cost *plus operating costs* (heating, cooling, etc.), plus the annual cost of maintaining the house. As an old tutor and builder once told me, one has to look at a planned expenditure and decide: does it cost, or does it pay? On this basis, the all-wood log or timber house may be the best long-term investment bargain.

It is often estimated that the completed log house may cost double the catalog price. Others estimate that the final total cost may run closer to 2½ times the kit or package price. One consideration is that if you build with a total exposed wood interior, with no plaster or wallboard that needs painting, long-term interior maintenance costs can be held near

Before Painting

To avoid lap marks it is impor- into parts which end on logical etc. For best results, follow the tant to divide the substrate breaks such as doors, windows, procedures in diagram #2.

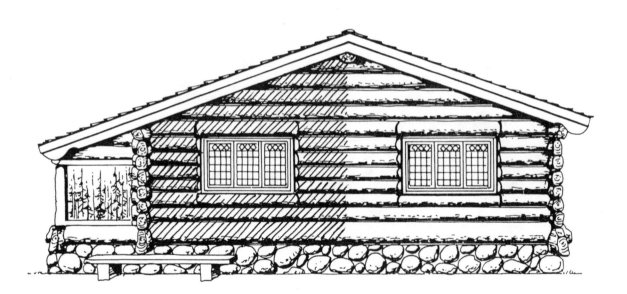

Incorrect Method   Diagram #1

Courtesy of Sikkens Woodfinishes.

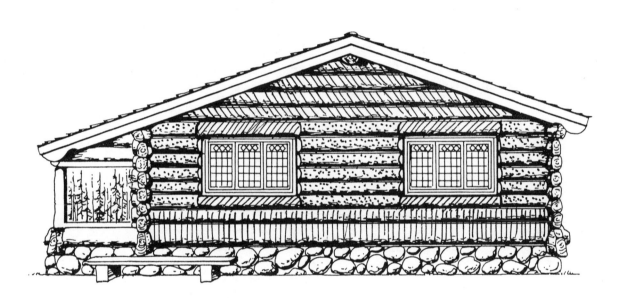

Correct Method   Diagram #2

Step #1		Paint The Top Section First
Step #2		Paint Between The Windows
Step #3		Paint The Bottom Section
Step #4		Paint The Trim

Courtesy of Sikkens Woodfinishes.

zero. But today's buyer often decides that a mix of plastered or painted walls or ceilings, along with generous amounts of wood, provides the best compromise.

LOG HOME INTERIORS

It used to be that one bought a log home because it had the wood look on both the exterior and the interior. Today, many people who build new log or timber homes elect to build interior partitions and/or ceilings with plaster or wallboard finishes. This mixing of the wood look, usually but not always preserved on the exterior walls, with the more contemporary plaster or wallboard finish permits the owner to have greater latitude in decorating. Having some walls or ceilings of wallboard/plaster permit the owners to mix textures, colors, and even fabrics, in the form of wall coverings, into the decorating scheme. This mix of many materials was once considered verboten in decorating etiquette. Not only is the mix encouraged and approved today, but the results can be extraordinary. For examples of what we mean, see Chapter 8, Decorating and Furnishing the Wood Home.

Wood Areas

Wood areas, such as ceilings, that require minimum cleaning can be left unfinished. Unfinished wood may darken with age, or may be soiled by wood smoke if you use a fireplace or wood stove. New wood ceilings can be left unfinished: A finish can be applied to the bare wood later if you find it necessary.

Bare wood, such as interior walls, that is subject to traffic may absorb moisture, smoke, or dirt. Once the wood has absorbed any staining material, and the stain is deep down, it will become very difficult to clean the surface. It is best to seal interior wood surfaces as quickly as possible to prevent staining and ensure future ease of cleaning. Ask your log home dealer to suggest an interior sealer for your home, and follow his instructions regarding application and any recommended waiting period. Or

consult the chart on "Finishing Log Interiors," prepared by Sikkens Woodfinishes. Sikkens' 800 number is listed in the Buyers' Guide at the end of this chapter.

One recommended finish technique involves application of a product called Penetrol to the entire interior wood surface. The product is water-like in consistency, and can easily be sprayed on interior walls or ceilings. The manufacturer recommends that two coats of Penetrol be applied, "wet on wet," with sprayer, brush, or roller. The term "wet on wet" means that one should apply a first coat of Penetrol and let that first coat soak in until the finish is dull, but not completely dry. As soon as the first coat of finish is absorbed into the wood, immediately apply the second coat. This application technique will help to seal the wood surface so that dirt and smoke will not be absorbed into the wood fiber and be difficult to remove. Penetrol is made by the Flood Company. For the name of your nearest Flood products dealer call or write:

The Flood Company
P.O. Box 399
Hudson, OH 44236-0399
(800) 321-3444

In Canada, contact:
The Flood Paint Specialty Company, Ltd.
2320 Harbour Road
Sidney, British Columbia V8L 2P6
CANADA

The Flood Company also makes a variety of other excellent products for use on exterior log and other wood surfaces.

Another natural wood finish product for finishing log home interiors is Lifeline Interior by Perma-Chink Systems Inc. Lifeline Interior forms a breathable finish that protects the wood surface while letting natural wood moisture escape from the wood. The tough protective film surface is easily cleaned and dusted, and prevents absorption of dirt and odors into the wood. For more information on Lifeline Interior or other log home products, call Perma-Chink Systems Inc. at (800) 548-1231.

LOG HOME EXTERIORS

The Log Homes Council points out that when wood is properly protected it is a most durable material. Wood artifacts found in 5,000-year-old Egyptian tombs, items that have been protected by the dry climate inside the tombs, are found to be perfectly preserved. Wood decay occurs only when the wood is attacked by oxygen, moisture, sunlight, and insects, all of which act to break down the wood's cellulosic fiber. But when man inserts a chemical barrier between the wood and the elements that attack it — air, water, sunlight, or insects — wood can be preserved so it will last for hundreds of years. The chemical barriers act as mildewcides, insecticides, herbicides, and fungicides to protect the wood from attack by the decay agents mentioned.

Protecting from Moisture

It is important to keep moisture away from logs because fungi that cause wood rot will thrive only if the moisture content of the wood reaches 30 percent or more. This means that the moisture/water repellent used to protect the wood must not only block out rain and snow, but also form a barrier against high humidity and even the morning dew.

According to the Log Homes Council, three factors work together to preserve and maintain your log home: basic design, periodic use of a wood preservative, and periodic use of an exterior penetrating finish (stain). Note also that, although this guideline is mentioned in the context of log or timber homes, the advice is just as sound for protecting any wood-sided house.

Basic Design

To ensure good preventive maintenance, choose a log home design that protects the structure from overexposure to sunlight, soil, and rain. A properly constructed foundation will support the logs so they are not in direct contact with the ground. It is important to be sure that the logs avoid ground contact because logs in direct ground contact are exposed to continuous moisture and to easy access by insects such as termites. The roof of the house should be properly flashed to prevent water entry into attic or ceiling areas. A roof with a wide overhang or eaves soffit will help shelter the walls of the house from attack by direct sunlight and from driven rain. Porches with wide roofs also help to shade and protect the exterior surfaces of the house, as well as enhancing energy efficiency by blocking summer rays and wintry blasts from direct contact with walls.

Wood Preservatives

The effectiveness of wood preservatives varies widely by climate, wood species, exposure, pigmentation, moisture content, and orientation of the house. A good wood preservative should be applied when the house is constructed, followed by a second application within six to eighteen months. The preservative should be renewed every four or five years, depending on the factors cited. Follow your manufacturer's recommendation for frequency of application for preservatives.

Exterior Finish

The log house should be allowed to weather for at least six months before any exterior finish is applied. This weathering process is intended to let the moisture inside the green wood dry out, while increasing the absorption rate of the final finish. However, the logs should be treated with wood preservatives (see above) to repel moisture and protect the logs during the entire weathering process.

Most log products are chemically treated by the manufacturer, so the logs will resist attack from insects and/or fungi. First, the logs are treated with zinc napthenate to control stain fungi. Then the logs are dipped into a borate solution to protect the logs against insects or fungi. Most of the moisture gained during this process is given up during storage and shipment, before the logs are erected at the building site.

Finishing Log Exteriors

Steps	EXTERIOR SYSTEM New Logs — Weathered, air or kiln dried, or wet/green logs after 6 months
#1.	Wet, by spraying the entire wood surface with water. Spray the surface with a solution containing a mixture of four ounces of trisodium phosphate (TSP) dissolved in one quart of bleach and three quarts of water. Apply with a garden sprayer. Let it "work" for 15-20 minutes. Power wash (not to exceed 500 psi) with clean water.
#1-A.	*If, after Step 1, there is still discoloration by blue fungi or nail run stains*: Spray the surface with a solution containing a mixture of 1/4 pound of oxalic acid crystals dissolved in one gallon of water. Apply with a garden sprayer. Let it "work" for 15-20 minutes. Power wash (not to exceed 500 psi) with clean water.
#2.	Allow the wood surface to dry for three days.
#3.	*If an area of high humidity and warm temperatures*: Apply one coat of Sikkens Wood Preservative, using a brush, roller, or sprayer.
#4.	Apply three coats (all within 30 days) of Cetol HLS, allowing 16 hours dry time between coats. Apply with a long hair, black China natural bristle brush.
#4-A.	*If the logs present much checking (mini)*: Apply two coats of Cetol HLS, followed with a top coat of Cetol Filter 7. By doing this, you can minimize water leaking through the checks.

Steps	EXTERIOR SYSTEM Previously Painted Logs — Old paint system
#1.	Remove all old coatings with a chemical, wax-free paint remover and power wash (not to exceed 500 psi) with clean water. Note: Aggregate blasting is very effective in removing the old paint system, but by its nature, it should be attempted only by a skilled professional.
#1-A.	*If, after Step 1, there is still discoloration by blue fungi or nail run stains*: Spray the surface with a solution containing a mixture of 1/4 pound of oxalic acid crystals dissolved in one gallon of water. Apply with a garden sprayer. Let it "work" for 15-20 minutes. Power wash (not to exceed 500 psi) with clean water.
#2.	Allow the wood surface to dry for three days.
#3.	*If an area of high humidity and warm temperatures*: Apply one coat of Sikkens Wood Preservative, using a brush, roller, or sprayer.
#4.	Apply three coats (all within 30 days) of Cetol HLS, allowing 16 hours dry time between coats. Apply with a long hair, black China natural bristle brush.
#4-A.	*If the logs present much checking (mini)*: Apply two coats of Cetol HLS, followed with a top coat of Cetol Filter 7. By doing this, you can minimize water leaking through the checks.

Finishing Log Interiors

Steps	INTERIOR SYSTEM New logs with a moisture content of less than 18%
#1.	In case of excessive resin, remove by applying heat (by means of a hot air gun) and scrape off the residue with lacquer thinner or liquid sandpaper.
#2.	Sand the surface with 100-200 grit sandpaper in the direction of the grain.
#3.	Vacuum or dust off.
#4.	Apply two coats of Cetol TS Interior with brush, roller, or sprayer.
#4-A.	*In case of hard wear (or on very porous substrates)*: A three-coat application is recommended.
#4-B.	Soft woods will often allow for uneven absorption of a finish that can lead to a blotchy appearance of the color. To prevent this problem, apply as a pretreatment, one coat of Sikkens Wood Conditioner. Brush on, wait 5-10 minutes, and wipe off with a lint-free cloth. Allow to dry 15 minutes and finish with Cetol TS Interior.

Steps	INTERIOR SYSTEM Previously varnished or stained logs
#1.	Sand the surface with 100-200 grit sandpaper in the direction of the grain until the surface is dull (without a gloss).
#2.	Vacuum or dust off.
#3.	Apply two coats of Cetol TS Interior with brush, roller, or sprayer.
#3-A.	*In case of hard wear (or on very porous substrates)*: A three-coat application is recommended.
#3-B.	Soft woods will often allow for uneven absorption of a finish that can lead to a blotchy appearance of the color. To prevent this problem, apply as a pretreatment, one coat of Sikkens Wood Conditioner. Brush on, wait 5-10 minutes, and wipe off with a lint-free cloth. Allow to dry 15 minutes and finish with Cetol TS Interior.

This log home exterior mixes a log/chinked joint effect at front, and a clapboard siding look at the back. Courtesy of Appalachian Log Homes.

The heavy wood look of this interior is accented by attractive chinking at log joints.
Courtesy of Appalachian Log Homes.

Maintenance

After the log house is erected, the owner should follow a three-step maintenance procedure. First, the logs must be cleaned. Next, the logs should be coated with a wood preservative that will protect the logs during any recommended weathering/drying period. When the recommended weathering period has passed, the logs should be finished.

Keep in mind that log houses often are built as remote retreats, and are often sited in areas where moisture problems are severe: in deep, damp woods or forests, or in high humidity areas alongside lakes, rivers, or oceans. This siting can adversely affect the log house, so that more frequent attention to recoating is required. If you choose to use exterior varnish, do not do so on an entire wood home. Use varnish (if at all) only on a small surface, such as a door, where frequent maintenance will not be an overwhelming problem.

Cleaning the Log Exterior

The following advice for cleaning log house exteriors is provided by the National Association of Home Builders.

1. You can clean the log exterior with a commercial wood cleaning product such as Wood Renew by Darworth, or Dekswood by the Flood Company. Or make a homemade cleaning solution to use for cleaning the logs. Dissolve four ounces of Savogran TSP-PF (phosphate free) or low-phosphate detergent in a solution of one quart of chlorine bleach and three quarts of water. This formula makes one gallon of cleaner; you will need one gallon of cleaner per 250 square feet of surface to be cleaned. Use clear water, applied with a power washer or hose nozzle to flush the chemicals away. Before applying the cleaner, cover any nearby plants or flowers with plastic film to protect them from the chemicals used during the cleaning process.

Before applying the cleaning solution to the logs, pre-wet the log surface(s) by spraying them with water from a garden hose nozzle or with a pressure washer. Let the water soak fifteen minutes or more, to wet and loosen any dirt and grime on the surface.

Then apply the cleaner solution. Wait until any discoloration on the logs begins to lift. When the grime has started to lift, power wash the logs using a washer with up to 500 pounds of pressure. Use this cleaning procedure on either new or old log surfaces to remove fungi, dirt, and air pollutants. Repeat the procedure if necessary to be sure the logs are absolutely clean, then rinse with clear water and let dry before proceeding.

2. When the logs are clean and dry, apply one or two coats of wood preservative. Preservatives available include Wolman Clear, Flood Seasonite, Sikkens Wood Preservative, Perma-Chink's Bora Care, and Chapman Wood Guard. Follow the log home dealer's instructions, as well as observing the label instructions on your chosen wood preservative product. An airless paint sprayer, rented from a tool rental outlet, can be a fast and efficient tool for applying the preservatives or finish stains. Note also that some of these wood preservatives are thin — the consistency of water — and can be sprayed onto the logs using an ordinary pump-type garden sprayer.

3. Let the log house weather for a few months, usually six months or more, following the manufacturer's recommendations. Then select a finish product to meet your own tastes.

Preserving Natural Wood

To preserve the natural wood color, use a transparent wood treatment such as Flood CWF or Aquatrol; Weatherall Log Guard: Wolman Raincoat; Perma-Chink's Lifeline Exterior; or Chapman Wood Guard. To add color without covering the wood grain, use Olympic Semi-transparent Stain; Pigmented Wood Guard; Pigmented Log Guard; or Wolman Raincoat with Natural Wood Toner.

In most cases, finish products that leave a protective film on the surface, such as paint or varnish, are not recommended as a finish on log houses, because logs may shrink considerably as they weather and dry out. One estimate is that, when green logs are used, the logs will shrink by as much as $1/16$, or just over six percent, as the house "settles." This much

This house exterior features a fully chinked log look. Log homes once were chinked. With today's tongue-and-groove milling, a tight wall is possible without chinking if the buyer prefers. Courtesy of Appalachian Log Homes.

Loft photo demonstrates the chinked look of the walls vs. the unchinked plank and beam ceiling.
Courtesy of Appalachian Log Homes.

shrinkage in the logs will, of course, result in cracking and peeling of any protective paint or varnish film. Also, the irregular surface of the log exterior makes future maintenance tasks such as paint sanding or scraping much more difficult than sanding or scraping flat siding. To avoid these future maintenance problems, it is best to avoid paint and varnish, and select instead a transparent wood treatment or a pigmented or semi-transparent stain as mentioned above. These products provide protection by being absorbed into the wood, rather than forming an inflexible protective surface film as paints or varnishes do.

If you already have failing paint, urethane, or varnish on a log building exterior and you wish to remove it, try Big Bare™ Log Coatings Remover. For the name of a dealer near you, contact Sashco in Commerce City, CO at (800) 767-5656. Another such product is Perma-Chink's Step Two. Call Perma-Chink at (800) 546-1231.

CHINKING LOGS

The founding fathers, who built log houses by simply stacking logs atop one another, in the cold North had to fill the inevitable cracks between the poorly fitted logs to keep out wintry drafts. To do this they usually "chinked" the cracks by stuffing hay or pine twigs into the cracks, then coating over the filler with clay (the clay and twig mixture was called wattle) to seal the cracks completely against the weather. In the South, where summer heat was the greater thermal concern, the cracks between logs were often left unchinked so that any passing breeze could enter and cool the interior.

Today's manufactured log houses have tongue-and-groove edges that fit tightly together, so chinking is no longer required to stop air infiltration on many log houses. But the chinking both provides a weather-tight seal against wind and water and yields a decorative effect in texture and color contrast with the logs, so many people choose to chink the log joints for these reasons.

Perma-Chink is a flexible, textured chinking and sealant, and it is the largest selling chinking product in the world. It looks and feels like traditional sand and mortar chinking, but it resists cracking and adheres more tightly to the logs than ordinary mortar chinking. The chinking is elastomeric, meaning that it cures but does not harden, so the chinking will stretch and shrink (rather than cracking) as the logs expand and contract with changes in the temperature and humidity. Perma-Chink is available in five-gallon pails and also in either 11-ounce or 30-ounce caulk tubes. It comes in six standard colors: white, tan, light grey, medium grey, brown, and sandstone.

Also available is Trap Rod, a spongy backing material used to fill joints or cracks between logs and to provide a smooth application surface for Perma-Chink. Trapezoidal in shape, Trap Rod is available in thicknesses varying from 3/4 inch up to 2 inches. Smaller round backer rod is available in 1/4-inch, 3/8-inch, and 1/2-inch diameters.

If your chinking begins to look a little the worse for wear and weather, try renewing chinking with Perma-Chink's Chink Paint. Chink Paint is a flexible latex paint intended to renew weathered chinking or to change the chink color. It is available in the same colors as Perma-Chink (above).

Cracking and Checking

Because it is exposed to extremes of weather, wood is prone to crack or check, especially along the grain lines. Most cracks in logs occur on the sides of the house that suffer the greatest exposure to wind and rain — the south and west sides. Checkmate™ is Perma-Chink's answer to filling checks or cracks in logs, timbers, or wood siding. Checkmate combines the properties of a caulk with those of a waterproof adhesive to provide a superior sealer for both checks and cracks. Also available for sealing small cracks both inside and outside is Perma-Chink's QSL, a log home sealant/caulk for use on corners, windows, door jambs, butt joints (end joints where logs butt together), sills, baseboards, and bathroom or kitchen fixtures.

BUYER'S GUIDE

Following is a list of manufacturers and/or suppliers of products needed to clean, finish, protect, and maintain log or timber homes. Note, however, that these products can also be used for cleaning and maintaining wood siding and many other outdoor wood structures such as decks, timber retaining walls, gazebos, and storage buildings. Call or write any of these companies to obtain catalogs or for further information.

Chapman Chemical Company
P.O. Box 9158
Memphis, TN 38109
(901) 396-5151
(800) 238-2523
Product: Oil preservative finish

The Flood Company
P.O. Box 399
Hudson, OH 44236-0399
(800) 321-3444
Products: Penetrol, Seasonite, CWF, Aquatrol

In Canada:
The Flood Paint Specialty Co., Ltd.
2320 Harbour Road
Sidney, British Columbia V8L 2P6
CANADA

Olympic
PPG Architectural Finishes, Inc.
One PPG Place
Pittsburgh, PA 15272

Perma-Chink Systems, Inc.
Western Division
17455 NE 67th Court
Dept. NWL92
Redmond, WA 98052
(800) 548-1231
Products: Perma-Chink, Chink Paint, Trap Rod, Bora-Care, Lifeline Interior, Lifeline Exterior, Wood Renew, Checkmate

Perma-Chink Systems, Inc.
Eastern Division
1605 Prosser Road
Knoxville, TN 37914
(800) 548-3554

Sashco
3900 E. 68th Avenue
Commerce City, CO 80022
(800) 767-5656
Products: Caulks, Big Bare™ Paint Remover

Schroeder Log Home Supply
1707 West Highway 2
P.O. Box 864
Grand Rapids, MN 55744
(800) 359-6614
Products: All log home maintenance products plus custom rustic furniture

Sikkens Woodfinishes
Akzo Coatings Inc.
1696 Maxwell Street
Troy, MI 48084
(313) 643-4995
(800) 833-7288
Products: Wood preservative, exterior and interior log finish products

This beautiful rural retreat, a log home set by a river, would be a perfect selection for the poet's "Vagabond's House." Courtesy of Appalachian Log Homes.

The double doors with sidelights and tiled floor with Persian rug make a perfect entry to welcome guests. Courtesy of Lindal Cedar Homes, Inc.

Another attractive entry idea. Natural wood door stain is framed by the light gray wash on the log walls and beams. Indian rugs add bright colors; the antique deacon's bench is a perfect seat for donning house shoes. Courtesy of Appalachian Log Homes.

Beamed ceiling, wood floor, durable leather chairs, and dark-stained wood cabinets/bookshelves provide an attractive setting. Note use of detail furnishings such as dolls, books, and ship's models to complete the picture. Again, undraped windows frame the view beyond, bringing the outdoors inside. Courtesy of Lindal Cedar Homes, Inc.

An eclectic blend of knotty cedar paneling and ceiling planks, the texture of stone in the fireplace and the overstuffed furniture result in a room that appears cozy and bright. Note the undraped windows overlooking the porch and the view beyond. Courtesy of Lindal Cedar Homes, Inc.

Plush sofa and chair, multicolor throw pillows, brass fireplace tools and ceiling fan, a unique wooden wall clock; a coffee table with cup, grapes, an open book; an antique rocking chair, a guitar, duck decoys ... on a clear day, you can see forever. Courtesy of Lindal Cedar Homes, Inc.

The bird's eye view accentuates the soaring beamed ceiling. This seaside retreat has a white ceiling fan, white-painted window trim, and privacy shutters. Notice the white chinking between gray logs and rope and post stair rail design. The natural wood tones of the furniture and floors offer an attractive contrast. Courtesy of Appalachian Log Homes.

Note the contrast between the various wood shades featured in the ceiling planking, truss beams, floor, loft railings, door, and kitchen cabinets. Off-white chinking between logs provides visual relief. Courtesy of Appalachian Log Homes.

Stone, brass, wicker, and glass accent the many wood tones. Note the brass four-poster bed, the ruffled lace curtains, and the area rugs over pegged wooden floors. Courtesy of Appalachian Log Homes.

At right, a wall-hung crank telephone, a bouquet of garlic buds, a wicker laundry basket filled with silk flowers, wide plank floors, and a gleaming antique cookstove provide the finishing touches for this paneled and beamed room. Courtesy of Lindal Cedar Homes, Inc.

White plaster walls and cabinets contrast with the stained plank and beam ceilings, the doors, and the natural wood finish of the stools, table, and chairs. Note the roof window shafts in wood, and the recessed lights in the kitchen ceiling. Courtesy of Lindal Cedar Homes, Inc.

The knotty tongue-and-groove wall and ceiling panels contrast with the darker kitchen cabinets, the gray slate-like countertops, and the black appliances. Courtesy of Appalachian Log Homes.

The light wood tones of the furniture, flooring, and ceiling planks contrasts with the dark wood of the log walls and beams. Extensive use of glass, including round windows over doors and roof windows, makes the interior light and livable. Note the contrast of the wood with the white china in the open china cabinet. Courtesy of Lindal Cedar Homes, Inc.

Soaring ceilings, beams and trusses, chinked log walls, and expanses of glass provide so much visual appeal that few furnishings are needed to complete this sportsman's retreat. Furnishing are sparse and simple: trophy elk and deer heads are on one wall, with a mounted tiger at left. Courtesy of Appalachian Log Homes.

This loft overlooks the living room. Ceiling planking is washed with a white stain; beams are light gray. Color and contrast are introduced via bright Indian rugs, bright wood stain on chair and cabinet, and brass ceiling fan and lamps. Courtesy of Appalachian Log Homes.

The large picture window over sink and roof window above the cooktop island make this kitchen light and airy. Wood cabinets contrast with the white painted walls and white laminate countertops. Lots of green plants and a fruit basket complete the accessories list. Courtesy of Lindal Cedar Homes.

7.

Fireplaces and Wood-Burning Stoves

By the fireplace where the fir logs blaze
And the smoke rolls up in a weaving haze.
I'll want a wood-box, scarred and rough,
For leaves and bark and odorous stuff
Like resinous knots and cones and gums
To chuck on the flames when winter comes.
And I hope a cricket will stay around
For I love its squeaky lonesome sound.

According to the Wood Heating Alliance (WHA), the fireplace is the most appealing amenity for prospective home buyers in the over $100,000 category; approximately 78 percent of American home buyers seek a fireplace as a preferred special feature. Further, the WHA notes that fireplaces and wood-burning stoves are not for mere decorative effect. Forty percent of wood burned is burned for primary or supplementary residential heating. Little wonder that modern Americans echo the thoughts of Thomas Jefferson, who wrote that "The happiness of the domestic fireside is the first boon of Heaven."

HISTORY

Think of a log or timber home. When you are reflecting on these two types of homes, what is the next thought that springs into mind? Chances are that this word association game might conjure up visions of a cheery fireside, either before a wood-burning stove or in front of a fireplace. Young Abe Lincoln, we are told, while studying in his log abode, did his "sums," or arithmetic, by the light of a fireplace, using a piece of chalk to write the numbers on the back of a shovel. The scene has been repeated in hundreds of frontier movies: John Wayne lit his cigarettes from the fireplace, and ate, dozed, and with his leading ladies dreamed by the fireplace hearth of their future on the frontier. "A fireside is a great opiate," wrote British poet Leigh Hunt in *A Few Thoughts on Sleep*. The fireplace was not only the sole source of heat to warm the frontier log cabin, it also served to heat water for bath or laundry, and to cook the family's meals.

Many pieces of Early American furniture were even designed to be used at fireside. By the fireplace sat wingback chairs with backs that wrapped around the occupant, so the reflected heat could warm one while the chair back blocked off cold drafts. There are even antique tables available with adjustable tops so that when dinner is done the top pivots, the base of the table becomes a chair seat, and the tabletop not only doubles as a chair back, but it also is a reflector to bounce the heat waves back toward the occupant. Because of its many uses, the fireplace thus became the focal point of all family activities, becoming almost a symbol for family togetherness.

This free-standing gas fireplace has three sides in glass for a wider view of the fire.
The gas flame is adjustable, and the unit produces 20,000 to 31,000 Btu's per hour.
Courtesy of Heat-N-Glo Fireplace Products, Inc.

In old southern cabins, such as those seen at President Andrew Jackson's Tennessee estate, the Hermitage, you can see fireplaces with chimneys made of wood. It is small surprise that some of these fireplace chimneys actually caught fire, and the flames sometimes spread to engulf the cabins as well.

"CHIMNEY EFFECT"

Fireplaces and wood-burning stoves have changed much since the frontier days. Decades ago, when the fireplace was 100% masonry construction, we learned that, to a great degree, the usefulness of a fireplace depended on the skill of the mason who built the unit. A fireplace chimney operates on the principle that hot air rises, and that cool replacement air is pulled in to replace the rising heated air. This principle is called the "chimney effect," and is also employed to vent heated air out of house attics, and to cool houses using whole house fans.

To take advantage of this chimney effect, the draft is started by lighting quick-burning kindling or crumpled newspaper in the firebox. This not only gets the air heated so it begins to rise, pulling or "drafting" replacement air in behind it, but the fast-burning materials also warm the firebrick and chimney flue tile, keeping the chimney effect going and the home fires burning.

THE IMPORTANCE OF PROPER CONSTRUCTION

As we began to use better insulation, weather-stripping, and caulking, and as houses grew tighter, the fireplace draft could not pull in sufficient replacement air for combustion, the house would develop "negative pressure." The fireplace would smoke and the draft would fail. To avoid the failed draft and to ensure a sufficient supply of replacement air for combustion, most people would open a window or door. The trouble with this, of course, is that it is very wasteful of energy: one is trying to force the heated air to exit and cold air to enter the house. To reduce heat loss, today's fireplaces have ducts to pull in outside air for combustion.

If the fireplace opening is properly constructed, the top of the opening forms a bowl or dam to trap any smoke so it will not roll back into the room, but will be forced to rise up the chimney. If the mason is not sufficiently experienced, the fireplace will not "draw," or draft, properly. The logs will smolder, and smoke will fill the house rather than wafting up the chimney. The fireplace will then be useless for producing heat. The smoking and poor combustion will make having a fire in the fireplace a very disagreeable experience. The result of poor masonry craftsmanship is an expensive but useless fireplace. In the old days, fireplaces that would not function properly were quite common.

The Prefabricated Firebox

This Catch-22 feature of having a fireplace built was largely eliminated when the Heatilator company began to offer a prefabricated steel firebox that featured a built-in chimney damper. Using the Heatilator firebox unit, the steel firebox is positioned on the masonry fireplace foundation, and the brick or stone fireplace is built around it. As the masons progress and the masonry fireplace surround rises upward, clay chimney tiles are set atop one another to form the chimney, and a finish material, usually either brick or stone, is placed around the clay tiles. Then the mason covers the inside of the steel firebox with a lining of firebrick, brick specially tempered to withstand direct fire contact, and the finished fireplace unit is considered foolproof, assuming that you followed a few specific operating procedures. These procedures include burning seasoned wood, operating the unit properly — i.e., opening a window to ensure that combustion air is plentiful, or providing ducts to draw in outside combustion air — and cleaning the chimney regularly to eliminate soot and to remove creosote, thereby preventing dangerous chimney fires.

ENVIRONMENTAL CONSIDERATIONS

Just about the time we had fireplace construction and operation down to a science, the environmentalists decided that fireplaces and their chimneys were a source of energy loss and that wood smoke is a pollutant. Manufacturers went back to the old drawing board for more design reform on the fireplaces and wood stoves. Fireplaces were redesigned and are now built so that they draw their combustion air from outdoors, to avoid pulling the indoor heated air up the chimney and wasting the heat energy. Glass doors are closed so that indoor air that is already heated will not be wasted by being exhausted up the chimney. And, in some areas, gas fireplaces are offered to conform to strict regulations against burning wood. As an alternative, or often as a supplement to building a fireplace, consumers often choose one of the many modern wood-burning stoves available, such as the Jotul. These wood-burning stoves can be used either for heat alone or for both heating and cooking.

Another alternative is the pellet stove. Pellet stoves burn pellets made from wood scrap or sawdust. These stoves burn much cleaner than ordinary fireplaces and are EPA approved for emissions.

CHOOSING A FIREPLACE

When choosing a fireplace, the basic decision may come down to the budget available. This means making a decision of whether to have a traditional masonry unit, or to choose a less expensive prefabricated model instead. Prefabricated models have become popular because they can be installed without the need for expensive masonry foundations or masonry chimneys. These fireplaces are so constructed and insulated that they can be installed with "zero clearance"; i.e., the flames are controlled so that they need neither space nor masonry to be between the fireplace unit and the wood framing or other combustible materials around them. The lightweight prefab units can rest directly on the house subfloor (usually with only a layer of protective sheet metal between the hearth and the subfloor). They thus offer total flexibility of location. The fireplaces can be fitted with a Class A metal chimney that is a sort of metal pipe within a pipe; there

Heat-N-Glo is the first company to manufacture a direct vent, built-in gas fireplace, featuring easy installation with no chimney. AGA (American Gas Association) approved for LP or natural gas, with a rated input of 27,000 Btu's per hour.
Courtesy of Heat-N-Glo Fireplace Products, Inc.

Where standard wood-burning fireplaces are prohibited, the Heat-N-Glo Model CBS-41 (Clean Burn System) can be utilized. the unit passes all four phases of the EPA Phase II performance standards for residential wood heaters. The unit can burn up to 7 hours on 15 pounds of wood, and is up to 65 percent energy efficient.
Courtesy of Heat-N-Glo Fireplace Products, Inc.

is air space between the two chimney pipes. This construction ensures that the exterior surface of the metal chimney stays cool, and will not cause a fire when the chimney pipe comes into contact with wood or other combustible materials. The fireplace can be fitted with the metal chimney, covered with wood framing and a plywood enclosure called a "chase." The chase can then be covered with decorative brick or stone to simulate a traditional masonry fireplace, but at considerably less cost.

Cost Variables

What is the cost differential between a conventional masonry fireplace and a prefabricated or zero-clearance model? There are too many variables to make an intelligent cost comparison, short of getting competitive bids from contractors. For example, a masonry fireplace can have a limited amount of expensive surface brick or stone showing, so that the final cost can be quite modest. By the same token, one could choose a top-of-the-line prefabricated model, frame it in and build a plywood chase, and then cover the plywood with large amounts of expensive stone, brick, or ceramic tile, so that the final fireplace cost could be very high.

In addition to the basic masonry vs. prefabricated question, there are other variables that can affect fireplace costs. One variable is the quality (and price) of the stone, brick, or ceramic tile used, and the quantity involved. The amount of face or finish brick, stone, or ceramic tile might be limited to a total only of a pair of slim columns framing the fireplace opening. It might include the entire fireplace wall, covering perhaps several hundred square feet of area. Other fireplace options may include such items as remote hot air registers that can be mounted in the walls or floors — even in other rooms. Fireplaces having remote hot air registers also must have electric blower units to push the hot air to the remote vents or registers.

GAS FIREPLACES

Don't overlook the new gas fireplaces available. The gas fireplace can let you enjoy the comfort of a real fire at the flick of a switch — even by remote control that works just like your television channel selector. Gas fireplaces can be vented directly through a wall, like a clothes dryer, which eliminates the need for any chimney. This lets you install a gas fireplace almost anywhere in your house, even beneath a window. And if you don't have room to store firewood — or just hate the mess of bark and ashes — the gas fireplace is a useful option. Don't worry about giving up the authenticity of a real wood fire: gas fireplace logs can simulate natural woods such as birch, pine, or oak. The blaze can be adjusted to alter the color from the natural blue gas flame to a lustrous golden yellow.

SIZE OF THE FIREPLACE

Other fireplace options or choices available include choosing the size of the fireplace unit. A large "great room" area may cry out for a massive fireplace, the entire wall soaring to a cathedral ceiling reaching upward 15 feet or more, all covered with hundreds of square feet of stone or brick. If a fireplace is also wanted in the kitchen or dining area, one may choose a two-way fireplace that can be seen through the wall from two rooms. A cozy bedroom or den may need a smaller fireplace, perhaps a 36-inch model, to avoid overwhelming the smaller space. If you intend to actually use the fireplace to heat all or some of the space in your house, choose a fireplace that includes a blower motor and remote air ducts with registers to distribute the heated air.

WHERE TO FIND A FIREPLACE

To find the right fireplace, check the ads in home magazines to find a list of companies making fireplaces, and check the features, cost, and installation for the model that meets your needs. The fireplace manufacturer will direct you to the dealer nearest you. Also, check the Yellow Pages of the telephone book under "Fireplace Equipment — Retail" for the names and locations of fireplace showrooms near your home. Look for a partial directory of fireplace and wood stove manufacturers in the Appendix at the end of this book.

BUILDING YOUR OWN FIREPLACE

Should you try to build your own fireplace? It depends on both time available and your own particular skill level. Some folks may be all thumbs and must hire everything done. Others may be so handy that they are able to tackle any task successfully. I have learned never to say never, since I was an editor for a home magazine. For example, a young woman called me one day to ask a question about roofing. I asked her if she could describe the type of roof valley by a particular dormer, and she replied "Oh, yes, I'm looking at it right now: I'm sitting on the roof with a cordless phone." It is obvious that there are all levels of do-it-yourself skills out there, and each person must judge his or her own level and areas of expertise. A precautionary note: The masonry or face finish material used on a fireplace will receive close examination from family, friends, and future buyers of your home. Any workmanship that is less than expert will not only attract attention but will also detract from the quality effect you are trying to create.

Building a conventional masonry fireplace usually is best left to experienced masons. Still, a brochure titled "An American Dream: The Log Home" tells the story of a fellow who not only built his own two-story, 5,600-square-foot log house, but also built a walk-through fireplace. There is a second-floor room accessible via a wood gangway through the arched door opening in the fireplace chimney. The owner designed the unit himself, and engineers promptly announced that it could not be done. Working with a neighbor, the owner fabricated forms from steel, then wrapped the masonry around the steel forms. This is no small unit for roasting marshmallows, either. The hand-picked stones used in building the massive fireplace were gathered from a friend's Tennessee farm. The owner-builder did the work, with the help of neighbors. The two-story tall stone fireplace consumed four months of time and work and 21 tons of stone, but the results are well worth the cost and the effort. Could anyone duplicate this effort? Well, not just anyone; we would recommend that such projects be tackled only by those who are considered to be fairly versatile in their skills. Still, the financial rewards are considerable for those who can do, and the log house and fireplace should return a handsome profit on investment if the couple should ever decide to sell. Don't be too tempted by the vision of potential profits, however. Most log and timber homes end up being viewed as priceless family treasures, and few are found in the "House For Sale" columns. Owners simply do not want to part with them.

INSTALLING A PREFABRICATED FIREPLACE

If a log house is planned to have a conventional masonry fireplace on an outside wall, the manufacturer will leave a void or an opening in the wall at the designated fireplace location. This allowed space will accommodate the fireplace and chimney. If the fireplace is to be a prefabricated or zero-clearance model, allowances should be made in any ceiling, roof section, or wall through which the metal chimney should pass. There is no need for extensive framing or wall alterations because of the minimum size and weight of the metal fireplace chimney. All that is needed is that holes be cut through any ceiling or wall, large enough to permit the chimney pipes to penetrate to the outside.

Most of these metal chimney pipes have an inner flue of stainless steel pipe, an outer galvanized steel wall, and a blanket of non-combustible mineral wool insulation between the two pipe walls. The stainless steel inside flue resists rust and burn-through, the outer wall of galvanized steel resists rust and corrosion, and the insulation blanket helps ensure that there is little or no heat transfer to the exterior pipe wall. This permits the "zero-clearance" installation in which there need be no space clearance for fire prevention between the metal chimney and the wood framing or other combustible building materials. By the same token, you should plan in advance for any wood-burning stoves you might install so that chimney placement can be part of the building plan, and the chimney(s) can be built to accommodate them.

Installation instructions for zero-clearance fireplaces may vary between different models and different

*A massive fireplace finished in manmade stone, located on an outside wall, can provide a
traditional masonry fireplace look at affordable cost.
Courtesy of Lindal Cedar Homes, Inc.*

Complete freedom of location permits this mid-wall mount, with open areas both above and below the firebox. Courtesy of Lindal Cedar Homes, Inc.

manufacturers. The basic instructions given here are general tips for your information. You should always read and understand the directions for installing your own particular unit.

The base units for zero-clearance fireplaces can usually be installed anywhere, over either wood or concrete floors. One point to remember when choosing the location for the fireplace is to position the unit so that the fireplace and exterior chimney will not interfere with any windows.

Some models call for a piece of sheet metal to be nailed to the subfloor, in front of the fireplace opening, as a guard against flying sparks starting a fire. At this point, the base section of the chimney pipe should be attached to the top of the fireplace unit. Do not tighten the chimney pipe connection to the fireplace until you are sure the chimney pipe is set at the proper angle. The chimney pipes are joined by turning the pipes counterclockwise, which locks the pipes together. At this time, you should also make the connection from the outside combustion air duct to the base unit.

The Fireplace Surround

After the fireplace unit is positioned, build a 2 x 4 frame wall around it. This 2 x 4 frame wall may be a simple U-shaped surround, or it may be as large as you wish — even a complete new wall. If the fireplace surround is to be a painted wall, you may use gypsum wallboard to cover the wall, to be taped and painted later. If you intend to cover the fireplace surround with manmade brick or stone, or ceramic tile, you may choose to cover the framed surround with Durock™, a base board product that is made of cement and reinforced with fiberglass fibers. Durock can be cut and nailed like wallboard. Attach brick, stone, or ceramic tile to the Durock surround, using the appropriate adhesive to secure the finish product to the Durock. Use a notched adhesive spreader or trowel to spread the adhesive on the Durock.

The Chimney

On the outside of the house, build a 2 x 4 frame of the desired dimensions to cover the metal chimney and to achieve the effect you want. This chimney surround, or "chase," can be just wide enough to cover the metal chimney, or it can be very wide to achieve a massive chimney effect. The exterior chimney chase may be covered with either exterior plywood or Durock backer board.

Check the manufacturer's instructions for the top or termination of the chimney and chase. Some manufacturers may recommend that for fire safety at least 2 feet of metal chimney must be left exposed above the top of the chase. There is a metal terminator or top that slips over the chimney pipe and covers the top of the chimney chase. There may be a collar that slips over the top of the chimney pipe and seals the crack between the chimney pipe and the metal terminator. The manufacturer may also include a spark arrestor to be fitted on top of the chimney pipe. This spark arrestor prevents flying sparks from exiting the chimney pipe and setting fire to the roof or other nearby objects.

To cover and finish the chimney chase, choose an adhesive and stone or brick covering product that is recommended for exposure to weather. To avoid adhesive or bond failure between the backer and the finish brick or stone, observe the application instructions on the adhesive. Be sure that the weather (temperature and humidity) is within the acceptable range for application of the adhesive.

WOOD-BURNING TIPS

There is some disagreement over the importance of drying or seasoning firewood prior to burning it. In the past, experts maintained that wood with a high moisture content produced excessive amounts of creosote, which in turn coated the chimney interior and might result in a future disastrous chimney fire. Some experts today say that if you maintain the fire at a steady rate of burn, you can control the amount of creosote and keep the chimney clean. Our advice is to do both: buy and use only seasoned firewood, and do not let the fire smolder, but keep a small fire burning at such a rate that the wood fuel is consumed at a brisk, steady, and clean-burning rate.

Today's zero-clearance fireplaces can be located almost anywhere, as demonstrated by this under-the-staircase installation. Courtesy of Heatilator Inc.

When installing your own fireplace, first lay out the stone on a canvas tarp to establish a pleasing pattern. Rubble or small stones should be placed randomly in the stone pattern to avoid having all the small stones in one area of the fireplace.
Courtesy of Heatilator Inc.

Another example of the flexibility possible with zero-clearance fireplace units.
Note brick hearth and plastered wall with brick accent around the fireplace opening.
Courtesy of Heatilator Inc.

Wood Weight/Density

The weight or density of wood varies widely by species. Heavy or dense woods include hickory, apple, white oak, red oak, and sugar maple, in that order. Lighter, less dense woods include (in descending order) white pine, balsam fir, cottonwood, and northern white cedar. By way of comparison, based on the total weight of 85 cubic feet of wood for each species, hickory wood weighs 4,327 pounds; red oak weighs 3,757 pounds; white pine weighs 2,236 pounds; and northern white cedar weighs only 1,913 pounds. Keep in mind that at 20 percent moisture content, any pound of wood contains about 6,400 Btu's of heat. You will see that there is about twice as much heat energy or Btu's in a pound of hickory wood as in a pound of white pine.

The denser or heavier wood will burn slowly, so that the burn rate is less efficient than the burn rate of the lighter woods. But the lighter woods may burn too intensely, producing high amounts of short-term heat. Check with your wood supplier. Experts often advise that you mix a few chunks of heavy or dense wood with some lighter wood, so that the lighter, fast-burning wood can help accelerate the burn rate of the denser woods. Speeding up the burn rate of the denser woods means they will produce less smoke, and therefore less creosote, as they burn. This will reduce creosote buildup in the chimney, reduce the possibility of dangerous chimney fires, and reduce the need for frequent chimney cleaning.

How Clean is Your Fireplace?

To check how clean your fireplace or stove is burning, keep an eye on the chimney. Do you see large amounts of thick smoke? That means that the wood you are using is burning too slowly, perhaps because the wood is too wet and needs seasoning, or perhaps because you are burning heavy, dense wood that tends to smolder and give off a lot of smoke. To reduce the amount of smoke to get a cleaner burn, keep the fire small, adding wood frequently for a brisk burn rate, rather than loading heavy wood onto the fire and letting the wood smolder and smoke.

CHIMNEY FIRES

We have referred several times to the danger of chimney fires. If excessive amounts of creosote build up in the chimney, the creosote can catch fire, and will burn with ferocious heat. The high heat may crack chimney flue tile, or burn through a metal chimney. This lets the fire damage or destroy the chimney. The fire then may spread to the house structure and burn down the house. If you use a fireplace or wood-burning stove frequently, have the chimney checked and/or cleaned frequently, perhaps once a year or more if you are so advised by a professional. For advice and chimney cleaning, contact a professional chimney sweep or the masonry contractor who built your fireplace (if no professional chimney sweep is available in your locality).

WOOD-BURNER FUEL OPTIONS

As already stated, the wood-burning appliance industry has spent a number of years and lots of research dollars to make wood-heating fireplaces and stoves more efficient, so that today's appliances not only get more Btu's of heat per burn, but also have reduced the pollution caused by using these appliances. The Wood Heating Education & Research Foundation (WHERF) states that today's new EPA-certified wood stove releases 3 to 6 grams of emissions per hour, compared to the old conventional wood stove emissions of 20 to 40 grams per hour. Wood-burning appliances are burning more cleanly by design. Today, according to the U.S. Census Bureau American Housing Survey of 1987, there are still 16,500,000 homes that heat with wood. This puts wood in third place in heating preference, compared to piped gas, first at 50,900,000 homes; electricity, second at 30,800,000 homes; and fuel oil, fourth at 14,800,000 homes heated. By cost per million Btu's, wood is $6.00 ($100 cord); natural gas is $8.00 ($0.60/therm); oil is $10.00 ($1.00/gallon); and electricity is $17.60 ($0.06/KwHr).

In light of these statistics, it is important to be sure that we not only select wood-heating appliances

A massive stone fireplace is a focal point in the design of this great room.
Courtesy of Heat-N-Glo Fireplace Products, Inc.

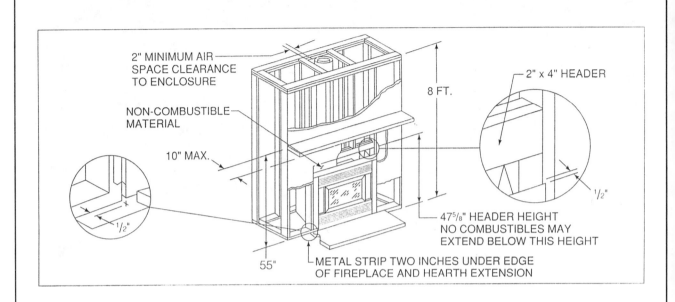

2" MINIMUM AIR
SPACE CLEARANCE
TO ENCLOSURE

NON-COMBUSTIBLE
MATERIAL

10" MAX.

8 FT.

2" x 4" HEADER

¹/₂"

47⁵/₈" HEADER HEIGHT
NO COMBUSTIBLES MAY
EXTEND BELOW THIS HEIGHT

55"

METAL STRIP TWO INCHES UNDER EDGE
OF FIREPLACE AND HEARTH EXTENSION

¹/₂"

Framing the fireplace.
Courtesy of Heatilator Inc.

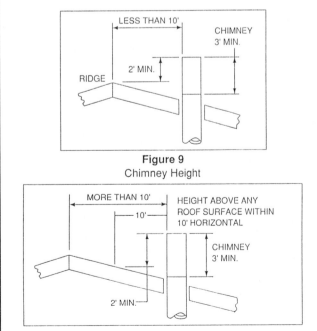

LESS THAN 10'

CHIMNEY
3' MIN.

2' MIN.

RIDGE

Figure 9
Chimney Height

MORE THAN 10'

10'

HEIGHT ABOVE ANY
ROOF SURFACE WITHIN
10' HORIZONTAL

CHIMNEY
3' MIN.

2' MIN.

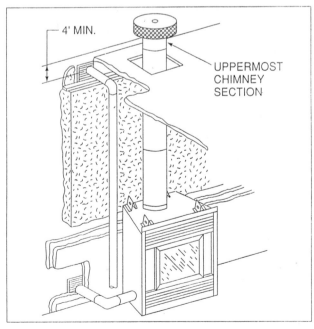

4' MIN.

UPPERMOST
CHIMNEY
SECTION

Outside air locations.
Courtesy of Heatilator Inc.

that are EPA-certified to be inherently efficient, but that we also choose our fuel carefully. We have already covered advice on what woods to burn, and how to achieve an efficient, clean burn in using wood. But there are also manufactured fuels that are proven to be clean and efficient alternatives to burning wood.

Keep in mind that the owner's manual supplied by the manufacturer of your fireplace or wood stove is always the best guide and the most complete source of information for using your own particular wood-heating appliance.

PELLET FUELS

The wood products industry in the past generated millions of tons of waste, in the form of useless wood chips and sawdust. Today, millions of tons of these wastes are manufactured into wood pellets and are consumed in special stoves and furnaces that are designed to burn the pellets. The wood pellets are about 1 inch long and $1/4$ inch in diameter and are packaged in plastic bags for convenient storage and handling. Normally sold by the ton, the wood pellets produce about 17 million Btu's of heat per ton.

For the home, pellet stoves are made as free-standing stoves or as fireplace inserts. The pellet stove produces heat in a different manner than an ordinary wood stove does. The conventional wood stove uses air flow controls to regulate the level of heat produced. Pellet stoves function with a constant flow of air, and the amount of heat derived depends on the amount of pellet fuel delivered to the combustion chamber. This small amount of wood pellets ensures that the fuel will burn with maximum efficiency, so you get a clean burn, with no ash, little smoke, and fewer safety problems.

Depending on the model of pellet stove or insert that you buy, you can have an appliance that has remote thermostats, complex computers, and circuit boards. Pellet stoves can be set up to hold several days' worth of fuel pellets, with the pellets fed automatically into the stove.

Like any appliance, pellet stoves require proper installation, operation, and maintenance. Seek out a knowledgeable dealer to help you with these important steps. For more information on pellet stoves contact:

Hearth Products Association
1101 Connecticut Avenue, NW, Suite 700
Washington, DC 20036

FIRELOGS

Firelogs are made by recycling sawdust particles and bonding them together with wax. The wax not only is the "adhesive" that bonds the sawdust together, it also is a supplementary fuel, helping to increase the burn to reach temperatures that result in almost complete combustion. Firelogs are much like candles, with the sawdust particles serving as the wick and the wax serving as the fuel. This means that both carbon monoxide and particulates are reduced to the minimum, to ensure very low emissions.

The Firelog Manufacturers Association commissioned an independent research laboratory to test the environmental impact of firelogs. The research company, Shelton Research Inc. of Santa Fe, New Mexico, tested for emission rates of carbon monoxide, particulates, and creosote accumulation. The tests prove that firelogs burn cleaner than cordwood. Fewer emissions, along with the convenience and cleanliness of packaged logs, provide ample reasons for the consumer to consider using firelogs. Members of the Firelog Manufacturers Association (FMA) and their products include:

Canadian Firelog Ltd.
(Hearthfire)

Conlen Industrial Corporation
(Northland and Sterno)

Duraflame, Inc.
(Duraflame and Cedarflame)

Monto Industries Ltd.
(Ultraflame and Flameglow)

Particulate Matter Emission Rate

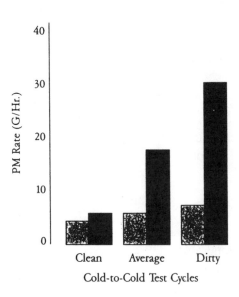

Carbon Monoxide Emission Rate

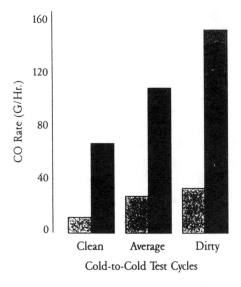

Creosote Accumulation Rate

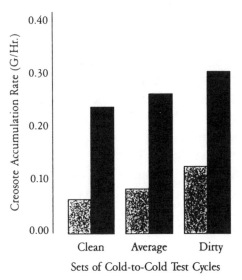

Courtesy of the Wood Heating Alliance.

Pine Mountain Corporation
(Pine Mountain and Golden Flame)

Sebring Forest Industries
(Amberglow)

8.
Decorating and Furnishing the Wood Home

All these things I will have about,
Not a one could I do without;
Cedar and sandalwood chips to burn
In the tarnished bowl of a copper urn,
A paperweight of meteorite
That seared and scored the sky one night ...

The hammers and saws are silent, the convoy of tradesmen's trucks has vanished down the lane, walls and roof are tight against the ravages of both rain and wind. Although that "new" smell of paint and other products lingers, and there are final adjustments to be made to drawers and hinges, the new house is at long last finished. It's time to begin the final phase of our grand adventure: decorating and furnishing the new home.

For some, this step of furnishing the house may be just another shopping chore. Some may choose to head out to the local furniture mart, checkbook or credit card in hand, to buy a houseful of furnishings to equip the new house. But for most of us, the fun of building the house is a prelude to an even more satisfying adventure. More than half the fun of building the dream house is in decorating and furnishing the house after the construction work is finished. We are not simply trying to fill space; we are trying to provide the perfect finishing touches to

this place we will call home, to make it finally and completely our own. We will move slowly and deliberately, choosing our furnishings piece by piece, the task a happy and satisfying fringe benefit to actually living in the new house.

We can eagerly spend years shopping furniture stores to find just the right overstuffed chair to fit that corner; touring antique shops for a unique set of brass fireplace tools; haunting art galleries to find a special picture to hang over the fireplace (we will know it's right when we see it); discovering the special bed quilt, with a million tiny hand stitches, painstakingly made by someone's grandma in a vine-covered cabin tucked away in the remote Smoky Mountains. Collecting the furnishings and final touches is perhaps the most satisfying part of the once-in-a-lifetime experience of building our dream home.

STYLE OF FURNISHINGS

When considering furnishings to complement a log or timber home, our first thoughts may be of the rustic style — Early American or Early Attic. We may well prefer rustic furniture as the proper complement to a traditional log home. Indeed, if our log or timber home is a vacation retreat, we may want to

This warm interior shows off a beautiful patchwork wall hanging as well as the owners'
holiday decorations. Courtesy of Gastineau Log Homes, Inc.

The skylights and exposed beams open up the upper portion of the great room.
Courtesy of Gastineau Log Homes, Inc.

keep things simple, inexpensive, and "bullet-proof"; i.e., sturdy enough to take all the abuse that is normal in such retreats. We may want to put our feet up on the coffee table, or use the sofa as a sleeping couch, or forgo rugs or carpeting in favor of easy-to-clean wood or vinyl flooring.

But given today's modern log and timber home styles, there is no single "right" approach to decorating. If the home is a seashore retreat, or even a secluded primary home, we may choose an open view from the windows, unimpeded by curtains or drapes. We may seek out custom-made rustic furnishings, or choose a heated water bed. We may choose a whirlpool bath for two, or select a clawfoot bath tub because of its antique look.

Wall Surfaces

Modern log home interiors may offer a flat interior side that simply looks like horizontal wood paneling. These flat interior walls may be left in wood tone or may be stained to any hue. Some may be painted; interior partition walls of log or timber homes are often built of wallboard and then painted or decorated with wall coverings. These interiors can be furnished in country rustic, contemporary, or traditional style, or can be an eclectic mix of the best of each.

Hiding Electronic Gear

One precaution: most professional designers are agreed that modern electronic gear clashes with the log or timber home interior. When the log house is built, the logs must be mortised (grooved) on the blind side so that all wiring is well concealed. Cabinets or shelving with doors can hold a television, VCR, and stereo equipment, so these most modern items are concealed from view when the doors are closed.

DO-IT-YOURSELF OR PROFESSIONAL DESIGNER?

The question of whether you should design and furnish your own home interior or hire professional design help depends on a number of factors. Your budget, taste, past experience, and available time are all factors that can affect your final decision.

Perhaps the most important of these questions is the one of taste. The problem is that most of those among us who have poor taste do not know it. I well recall a husband and wife team who suffered from that lack of good taste. He was a building contractor; she decorated the houses he built. The problem was, as one carpenter was heard to mutter, that "all her taste was in her mouth." The contractor/husband, whose taste was equally flawed, was proud of the job his wife was doing. To the end, she insisted on painting the garage door panels in two colors, checkerboard fashion. Right up to the day they filed for bankruptcy and the sheriff came to hold the sale, the dynamic duo was sure that it was the public who was at fault for not recognizing their decorating talents. The moral is to seek professional advice (or at minimum the advice of honest friends), if for nothing more than to confirm your own good taste.

Free Design Guidance

At the very least, before striking out on your own, you should take advantage of the many sources of free design guidance available. Home magazines, interior designers, and department and furniture stores all can provide professional and affordable guidance as you plan your interior design.

STARTING A DESIGN NOTEBOOK

Most designers advise that the first step toward getting your interior design together is to pore over the photo sections of decorating/design magazines, tear out photos that strike your designing fancy, and file them in a notebook. If you find a particular photo that illustrates a style or something that you definitely *dislike*, tear it out and file it, too. Knowing your dislikes can be a great help for any designer you hire. The notebook file of dislikes can help your professional designer avoid a process of elimination and help him or her cut directly to the styles and colors that please you most. Whether you decide to go it alone or to hire professional design help, the

This spacious great room is obviously a source of comfort and enjoyment for the owners.
Courtesy of Gastineau Log Homes, Inc.

The reproduction cast-iron cookstove adds lots of charm to this kitchen.
Courtesy of Gastineau Log Homes, Inc.

notebook can be a valuable aid and a constant reference to the design style that matches your own tastes.

To begin your roundup of magazines that feature interior design schemes for log and timber homes, contact *Muir's Log Home Guide* for back copies of their Special Decor issues. You can write them, or for a more immediate response call:

Muir's Log Home Guide
Muir Publishing Company, Inc.
164 Middle Creek Road
Cosby, TN 37722
(800) 345-LOGS (outside Tennessee)
(615) 487-2256
(800) 237-2643 (Ontario and Quebec)
(615) 487-3249 (FAX)

Other home decorating/design magazines that feature log and timber home interiors include *Country Living, Home*, and *Better Homes and Gardens*. You can find these and other decorator magazines on most newsstands.

DEPARTMENT STORES

Major department and home furnishings stores have interior designers on staff to assist their customers with design decisions. In my own home city of Minneapolis, Minnesota, Dayton's (a major department store) has a Western Lodge line, plus interior designers who offer free design help to Dayton's customers. You can call Dayton's at (612) 375-2200.

Another Minneapolis furniture store, Gabbert's, has a design staff whose specialty is vacation home decorating. The decorating advice is free to Gabbert's customers, but designers also are available on a consulting fee basis. Call Gabbert's at (612) 927-1500. Sears and JC Penney stores also offer interior design services.

PROFESSIONAL DESIGNERS

If you will inquire in your own city, or a major city nearby, you should be able to find an interior designer who can help guide your choices, or who, if you prefer, will take over the entire interior design project and execute it for you.

To begin your search, check the Yellow Pages of the telephone book under the heading "Interior Decorators & Designers." In my Minneapolis telephone book, there are fully two and a half pages of design firms listed, with dozens of interior designers to choose from. Also, check the book for the phone number of the District Chapter of the American Society of Interior Designers (ASID) and ask for a referral to a designer who has experience working with log or timber homes.

Cost for Professional Design Service

Interior designers have varying fee structures. Among these are charging a flat fee for the entire job, cost plus, and retail less. The flat fee is based on the number of hours it will take the designer to complete the job. You will find that hourly rates vary widely from one part of the country to another, and with the experience and popularity of the designer. You may find this arrangement the most economical if you need help with some facets of the job but are happy to do some legwork yourself.

Cost plus means that the designer purchases furnishings and materials at his or her net or wholesale cost, then charges you the cost plus a markup of anywhere from fifteen percent to one-third. This option lets you purchase below retail and gives you the services of an interior designer.

Retail less means that the designer charges you the retail price of the materials less a percentage, usually ten to thirty percent. This alternative is not necessarily recommended, however, because it has potential pitfalls. For example, let's say the designer purchases a $1,000 cabinet at his usual 50 percent discount. At retail less thirty percent, the cabinet would cost you $700; at cost plus thirty percent, it will cost you $650.

How much does professional design service cost? Here we go back to the advice my contractor/ mentor gave me years ago. Does it cost, or does it pay? Having worked in the housing business most of my life, it has always been my conviction that good professional design, whether from an architect, a landscape designer, or an interior designer, will return more than it costs. When you are talking of spending over $100,000, proper design is a small part of the budget. It has wisely been said that you will pay in frustration and dissatisfaction for poor housing design long after the dollar price has been forgotten.

Vagabond's House

As I stated in the Introduction, my entire working life has been spent either building or writing about housing. It should come as no surprise then that even my favorite poem would be about housing. The title of the poem is "Vagabond's House," and the author is Don Blanding, an Oklahoma-born vagabond who left home at a tender age to travel the world. Blanding's poetry was very popular with the flappers of the Roaring '20's who gathered on the beach at Waikiki. Blanding became the poet laureate of Hawaii.

Fifty years ago the poem "Vagabond's House" was the inspiration for a light-hearted movie called *Mr. Blanding Builds His Dream House*: a less sentimental, more realistic view of the problems and frustrations Blanding might encounter if he actually set about building a dream house. The movie was redone a few years ago as *The Money Pit*.

The Germans have a word for the urge to travel: *fernweh*, or a "longing for far places." Don Blanding had *fernweh* in abundance, and spent his life circling the globe. But like most of us who love to travel, Blanding also had the occasional attack of *heimweh*, or homesickness. The story is that one evening, while in a remote corner of the world, Blanding was thinking of all the things he loved but had missed by living the vagabond's life. Vagabonds leave behind family, lovers, friends, pets ... and home. Not least of these trade-offs in a vagabond's life is the forfeiture of possessions of any kind: vagabonds do not travel with books, pianos, or a favorite easy chair. So Blanding spent a few hours dreaming of the house he would build one day when he stopped wandering, his "Vagabond's House." We decided to include the poem in this book because, to my mind, no other words express so well the universal basic longing we all have for a familiar place to call home.

Vagabond's House

When I have a house ... as I sometime may ...
I'll suit my fancy in every way.
I'll fill it with things that have caught my eye
In drifting from Iceland to Molokai.
It won't be correct or in period style
But ... oh, I've thought for a long, long while
Of all the corners and all the nooks,
Of all the bookshelves and all the books,
The great big table, the deep soft chairs
And the Chinese rug at the foot of the stairs,
(It's an old, old rug from far Chow Wan
that a Chinese princess once walked on.)

My house will stand on the side of a hill
By a slow broad river, deep and still,
With a tall lone pine on guard nearby
Where the birds can sing and the storm winds cry.
A flagstone walk with lazy curves
Will lead to the door where a Pan's head serves
As a knocker there like a vibrant drum
To let me know that a friend has come,
And the door will squeak as I swing it wide
To welcome you to the cheer inside.

For I'll have good friends who can sit and chat
Or simply sit, when it comes to that,
By the fireplace where the fir logs blaze
And the smoke rolls up in a weaving haze.
I'll want a wood-box, scarred and rough,
For leaves and bark and odorous stuff
Like resinous knots and cones and gums
To chuck on the flames when winter comes.
And I hope a cricket will stay around
For I love its squeaky lonesome sound.

There'll be driftwood powder to burn on logs
And a shaggy rug for a couple of dogs,
Boreas, winner of prize and cup,
And Mickey, a loveable gutter-pup.
Thoroughbreds, both of them, right from the start,
One by breeding, the other by heart.

There are times when only a dog will do
For a friend ... when you're beaten, sick and blue
And the world's all wrong, for he won't care
If you break and cry, or grouch and swear,
For he'll let you know as he licks your hands
That he's downright sorry ... and understands.

I'll have on a bench a box inlaid
With dragon-plaques of milk-white jade
To hold my own particular brand
Of cigarettes brought from the Pharaoh's land
With a cloisonne bowl on a lizard's skin
To flick my cigarette ashes in.
And a squat blue jar for a certain blend
Of pipe tobacco. I'll have to send
To a quaint old chap I chanced to meet
In his fusty shop on a London street.

A long low shelf of teak will hold
My best-loved books in leather and gold
While magazines lie on a bowlegged stand
In a polyglot mixture close at hand.
I'll have on the table a rich brocade
That I think the pixies must have made
For the dull gold thread on blues and grays
Weaves the pattern of Puck ... the magic maze.
On the mantelpiece I'll have a place
For a little mud god with a painted face
That was given to me ... oh, long ago
By a Philippine maid in Olongapo.

Then ... just in range of an easy reach ...
A bulging bowl of Indian beech
Will brim with things that are good to munch,
Hickory nuts to crack and crunch,
Big fat raisins and sun-dried dates
And curious fruits from the Malay Straits,
Maple sugar and cookies brown
With good hard cider to wash them down,
Wine-sap apples, pick of the crop,
And ears of corn to shell and pop
With plenty of butter and lots of salt ...
If you don't get filled it's not my fault.

And there where the shadows fall I've planned
To have a magnificent Concert-Grand
With polished wood and ivory keys
For wild discordant rhapsodies,
For wailing minor Hindu songs,
For Chinese chants with clanging gongs,
For flippant jazz and for lullabies
And moody things that I'll improvise
To play the long gray dusk away
And bid good-bye to another day.

Pictures ... I think I'll have but three;
One, in oil, of a wind-swept sea
With a flying scud and the waves whipped white ...
(I know the chap who can paint it right)
In lapis blue and deep jade green ...
A great big smashing fine marine
That'll make you feel the spray in your face.
I'll hang it over my fireplace.

The second picture ... a freakish thing ...
Is gaudy and bright as a macaw's wing,
An impressionistic smear called 'Sin,'
A nude on a striped zebra skin
By a Danish girl I knew in France.
My respectable friends will look askance
At the purple eyes and the scarlet hair,
At the pallid face and the evil stare
Of the sinister beautiful vampire face.
I shouldn't have it about the place
But I like ... while I loathe ... the beastly thing
And that's the way that one feels about sin.

The picture I love the best of all
Will hang alone on my study wall
Where the sunset's glow and the moon's cold gleam
Will fall on the face and make it seem
That the eyes in the picture are meeting mine,
That the lips are curved in the fine sweet line
Of that wistful, tender, provocative smile
That has stirred my heart for a wondrous while.
It's a sketch of the girl who loved too well
To tie me down to that bit of Hell
That a drifter knows when he finds he's held
By the soft strong chains that passions weld.

It was best for her and for me, I know,
That she measured my love and bade me go
For we both have our great illusion yet
Unsoiled, unspoiled by a vain regret.
I won't deny that it makes me sad
To know that I've missed what I might have had.
It's a clean sweet memory, quite apart,
And I've been faithful ... in my heart.

All these things I will have about,
Not a one could I do without;
Cedar and sandalwood chips to burn
In the tarnished bowl of a copper urn,
A paperweight of meteorite
That seared and scored the sky one night,
A Moro kris ... my paperknife ...
Once slit the throat of a Rajah's wife.

The beams of my house will be fragrant wood
That once in a teeming jungle stood
As a proud tall tree where the leopards couched,
And the parrot screamed and the black men crouched.
The roof must have a rakish dip
To shadowy eaves where the rain can drip
In a damp, persistent tuneful way;
It's a cheerful sound on a gloomy day.
And I want a shingle loose somewhere
To wail like a banshee in despair
When the wind is high and the storm-gods race
And I am snug by my fireplace.

I hope a couple of birds will nest
Around the place. I'll do my best
To make them happy, so every year
They'll raise their brood of fledglings here.

When I have my house I will suit myself
And have what I'll call my "Condiment Shelf"
Filled with all manner of herbs and spice,
Curry and chutney for meats and rice,
Pots and bottles of extracts rare ...
Onions and garlic will both be there ...
And soyo and saffron and savory goo
And stuff that I'll buy from an old Hindu,

Ginger and syrup in quaint stone jars,
Almonds and figs in tinselled bars,
Astrakhan caviar, highly prized,
And citron and orange peel crystallized,
Anchovy paste and poha jam,
basil and chili and marjoram,
Pickles and cheeses from every land
And flavors that come from Samarkand.
And, hung with a string from a handy hook,
Will be a dog-eared, well-thumbed book
That is pasted full of recipes
From France and Spain and the Caribbees,
Roots and leaves and herbs to use
For curious soups and odd ragouts.

On the gray-stone hearth there'll be a mat
For a scrappy, swaggering yellow cat
With a war-scarred face from a hundred fights
With neighbors' cats on moonlight nights.
A wise old Tom who can hold his own
And make my dogs let him alone.

I'll have a window-seat broad and deep
Where I can sprawl to read and sleep,
With windows placed so I can turn
And watch the sunsets blaze and burn
Beyond high peaks that scar the sky
Like bare white wolf-fangs that defy
The very gods. I'll have a nook
For a savage idol that I took
From a ruined temple in Peru,
A demon-chaser named Mang-Chu
To guard my house by night and day
And keep all evil things away.

Pewter and bronze and hammered brass,
Old carved wood and gleaming glass,
Candles in polychrome candlesticks
And peasant lamps in floating wicks,
Dragons in silk on a Mandarin suit
In a chest that is filled with vagabond loot.
All of the beautiful useless things
That a vagabond's aimless drifting brings.

... Then when my house is all complete
I'll stretch me out on the window seat
With a favorite book and a cigarette
And a long cool drink that my cook will get
And I'll look about my bachelor nest
While the sun goes streaming down the west
And the hot gold light will fall on my face
And make me think of some heathen place
That I've failed to see ... that I've missed some way ...
A place that I'd planned to find some day,
And I'll feel the lure of it drawing me.
Oh damn! I know what the end will be.
I'll go. And my house will fall away
While the mice by night and the moths by day
Will nibble the covers off all my books
And the spiders weave in the shadowed nooks
And my dogs ... I'll see that they have a home
While I follow the sun, while I drift and roam
To the ends of the earth like a chip on a stream,
Like a straw on the wind, like a vagrant dream,
And the thought will strike with a swift sharp pain
That I probably never will build again
This house that I'll have in some far day.
Well ... it's just a dream house anyway.

Don Blanding
Vagabond Poet

Appendices

1. Log Homes Council Members

The 1970's brought the first public awakening to energy conservation and to a back-to-basics movement that was to spark the beginning of a rapid growth period in the log home industry. Soon afterward it became apparent that there was a need for a manufacturers' association to promote the benefits of log home construction.

The Log Homes Council (LHC) is a non-profit, voluntary national organization that represents more than sixty of the leading log home manufacturers. The LHC maintains a full-time staff in Washington, DC, where it is affiliated with the National Association of Home Builders and the Building Systems Council. The LHC sponsors research, training, and marketing programs and develops guidelines that guarantee the quality standards of the log home industry. Examples of the LHC's efforts are its support of the National Bureau of Standards' energy conservation study, which proved the energy efficiency of log homes; development of a log stress grading standard; and evaluation of national surveys conducted to help expedite log home financing. The members of the LHC work together to provide the public with quality products and services.

Log home companies produce factory-made or hand-crafted log homes with solid log walls ranging from 6 to 15 inches (or more) in thickness. Log homes are available in a variety of styles and designs, from hand-hewn to machine milled, and from classic country to upbeat contemporary. Styles of log homes vary greatly, and most manufacturers can custom-design homes for the buyer.

Members of the Log Homes Council have offices that are located from coast to coast, and demonstrate a commitment to quality products, high ethical standards, and professionalism. The following directory of members of the Log Homes Council lists the names, addresses, and phone numbers of member companies, along with the geographical areas served by each member company. Contact one of these companies with questions or for further information on builder-dealers in your particular area.

The address of the LHC is:

Log Homes Council
The National Association of Home Builders
15 & M Streets
Washington, DC 20005
(202) 822-0576

Members of the Log Homes Council

(Companies marked with ⚘ grade logs under an approved grading system.)

Air-Lock Log Company
Las Vegas, NM 87701
(505) 425-8888
(505) 425-8844 FAX
Market area: NM, AZ, CA, TX, UT, CO, NV

Alta Industries, Ltd.
Route 30, Box 88
Halcottsville, NY 12438
(914) 586-3336
(800) 926-2582
(914) 586-2582 FAX
Market area: Continental U.S. and Japan

American Timber Frame Structure
P.O. Box 226
187 W Kingston Springs Road
Kingston Springs, TN 37082
(615) 966-6440

Amerlink
P.O. Box 669
Battleboro, NC 27809
(919) 977-2545
(919) 442-6900 FAX
Market area: Worldwide

⚘ Appalachian Log Homes, Inc.
11312 Station West Drive
Knoxville, TN 37922
(615) 966-6440
(615) 675-2662 FAX
Market area: U.S. and export

🏠 Appalachian Log Structures, Inc.
I-77, Exit 132, Route 21S
P.O. Box 614
Ripley, WV 25271
(304) 372-6410
(800) 458-9990
(304) 372-3154 FAX
Market area: Continental U.S., Carribean, Far East, Europe, Canada, South America

Asperline
RD #1, Box 240
Route 150
Lock Haven, PA 17745
(717) 748-1880
(717) 748-1884 FAX
Market area: Worldwide

Authentic Homes Corp.
Box 1288
Laramie, WY 82070
(307) 742-3786
(307) 742-8536 FAX
Market area: U.S. and Japan

B.K. Cypress Log Homes, Inc.
P.O. Box 191
Bronson, FL 32621
(904) 486-2388
(904) 486-8075 FAX
Market area: U.S., Canada, Carribean

Beaver Mountain Log Homes, Inc.
RD 1, Box 32
Hancock, NY 13783
(607) 467-2700
(800) 233-2770
(607) 467-2715 FAX
Market area: U.S. and Japan

Brentwood Log Homes
427 River Rock Blvd.
Murfreesboro, TN 37129
(615) 895-0720
(615) 893-4118 FAX
Market area: Nationwide

Cedar Forest Products Company
107 W. Colden Street
Polo, IL 61064
(815) 946-3994
(815) 946-2479 FAX
(800) 552-9495
Market area: Nationwide

Cedar River Log Homes, Inc.
4244 West Saginaw Highway
Grand Ledge, MI 48837
(517) 627-3676
Market area: Nationwide

Century Cedar Homes, Inc.
P.O. Box 24013-306
Winston-Salem, NC 27114
(919) 922-2914
Market area: Nationwide & export

Colonial Structures, Inc.
7817 National Service Road
Suite 502
Greensboro, NC 27409
(919) 668-0111
(919) 668-7235 FAX
Market area: Nationwide

Country Log Homes, Inc.
Route 47 & Clayton Road
P.O. Box 158
Ashley Falls, MA 01222
(413) 229-8084
Market area: Northeast, Mid-Atlantic U.S.

Eastern Log and Timber Homes
P.O. Drawer 948
Summersville, WV 26651
(304) 872-5300
(304) 872-2909 FAX
Market area: Worldwide

🏠 Garland Homes by Bitterroot Pre-Cut
2172 Highway 93 North
P.O. Box 12
Victor, MT 59875
(406) 642-3095
(800) 642-3837
(406) 642-6643 FAX
Market area: U.S., Japan, Canada

🏠 Gastineau Log Homes, Inc.
Old Highway 54, Route 2
Box 248
New Bloomfield, MO 65063
(314) 896-5122
(800) 654-9253
(314) 896-5510 FAX
Market area: U.S., Japan, Korea, Holland, Finland, Belgium, Luxembourg

Greatwood Log Homes, Inc.
Highway 57
P.O. Box 707
Elkhart Lake, WI 53020
(800) 588-5812
(800) 242-1021
Market area: Continental U.S.

Green Mountain Log Homes
P.O. Box 428
Route 11 East
Chester, VT 05143
(802) 875-2163
Market area: Eastern U.S.

🏠 Hearthstone, Inc.
1630 E. Highway 25/70
Dandridge, TN 37725
(615) 397-9425
(800) 247-4442
(615) 397-9262 FAX
Post and beam homes
Market area: Worldwide

🏠 Heritage Log Homes, Inc.
P.O. Box 610
Gatlinburg, TN 37738
(615) 436-9331
(800) 456-4663
(615) 436-3923 FAX
Market area: U.S. and Europe

Hiawatha Log Homes, Inc.
M-28 East
P.O. Box 8
Munising, MI 49862
(906) 387-4121
(800) 876-8100
(906) 387-3239 FAX
Market area: Worldwide

🏠 Honest Abe Log Homes, Inc.
Route 1, Box 84
Moss, TN 38575
(615) 258-3648
(615) 258-3397 FAX
Market area: Nationwide

🏠 Jim Barna Log Systems
2679 North Alberta Street
P.O. Box 1011
Oneida, TN 37841
(615) 569-8559
Market area: Continental U.S. and Export

🏠 Kuhns Bros. Log Homes, Inc.
RD #2, Box 406A
Lewisburg, PA 17837
(717) 568-1422
(717) 568-1187 FAX
Market area: Continental U.S.

🏠 Lincoln Logs, Ltd.
Riverside Drive
Chestertown, NY 12817
(518) 494-4777
(800) 833-2461
(518) 494-7495 FAX
Market area: U.S., Japan, Korea, Canada, Europe

🏠 Lindal Cedar Homes, Justus Division
Box 24426
Seattle, WA 98124
(206) 725-0900
(206) 725-1615 FAX
Market area: Worldwide

Lodge Logs by MacGregor, Inc.
3200 Gowen Road
Boise, ID 83705
(208) 336-2450
(800) 533-2450
(208) 343-6490 FAX
Market area: Midwest and western U.S.

🏠 Log Cabin Homes, Ltd.
P.O. Drawer 1457
410 N. Pearl Street
Rocky Mount, NC 27802
(919) 977-7785
(919) 985-2810 FAX
Market area: Worldwide

🌲 Log Structures of the South
P.O. Box 470009
Lake Monroe, FL 32747
(407) 321-5647
(407) 831-5028 FAX
Market area: Nationwide

🌲 Lok-N-Logs, Inc.
P.O. Box 677, Rt. 12 South
Four Corners Road
Sherburne, NY 13460
(607) 674-4447
(800) 343-8928
(607) 674-6433 FAX
Market area: Continental U.S.

🌲 Majestic Log Homes, Inc.
P.O. Box 772
Ft. Collins, CO 80522
(303) 224-4857
(800) 279-5647
(303) 224-9879 FAX
Producer of full round hand-crafted log structures
Market area: Worldwide

🌲 Model Log Homes
75777 Gallatin Road
Gallatin Gateway, MT 59730-9702
(406) 763-4411
(406) 763-4414 FAX
Market area: U.S., Canada, Grand Cayman, Japan,
Korea

Montana-Idaho Log Corporation
995 South U.S. 93
Victor, MT 59875
(406) 961-3092
(406) 961-3093 FAX
Hand-crafted log homes
Market area: Nationwide

Moosehead Country Log Homes, Inc.
P.O. Box 268
Greenville Junction, ME 04442
(207) 695-3730
Market area: New England

Mountaineer Log Homes, Inc.
Moutaineer Blvd
Box 406
Morgantown, PA 19543
(800) 338-6346 (PA)
(800) 233-5147
Market area: Northeast & central eastern U.S.

🌲 Natural Building Systems, Inc.
P.O. Box 387
Keene, NH 03431
(603) 399-7725
(603) 352-5326 FAX
Market area: East coast and export

🌲 New England Log Homes, Inc.
2301 State Street
P.O. Box 5427
Hamden, CT 06518
(203) 562-9981
(800) 243-3551
(203) 782-2785 FAX
Market area: U.S., Canada, Japan, Korea, United
Kingdom

Newberry Building Systems Corp.
P.O. Box 101
Newberry, MI 49868
(906) 293-8283
(906) 293-3322 FAX
Market area: Michigan

North American Log Homes Systems & Country
Kitchens, Inc.
South 8680 State Road
Colden, NY 14033
(716) 941-3666
(800) 346-1521
Market area: Continental U.S.

🌲 Northeastern Log Homes, Inc.
P.O. Box 46
Kenduskeag, ME 04450-0046
(207) 884-7000
(800) 624-2797
(207) 884-7000 FAX
Market area: Worldwide

🌲 Northern Products Log Homes, Inc.
P.O. Box 616
Bomarc Road
Bangor, ME 04401
(207) 945-6413
(207) 945-9983 FAX
Market area: Continental U.S., Canada, Korea,
Japan

Phoenix Wood Products, Ltd.
Riverbend Log Homes
P.O. Box 411
Nackawie, New Brunswick E0H 1P0
(506) 575-2255
(506) 575-2855 FAX
Market area: Eastern U.S., Atlantic Canada, and
England

Pine Mountain Homes, Ltd.
P.O. Box 549
Spearfish, SD 57783
(605) 642-7940
(605) 642-3978 FAX
Hand-crafted and turned log homes from founda-
tion to turn-key
Market area: ND, SD, MT, NE, CO, WY

🌲 Pioneer Log Systems, Inc.
P.O. Box 226
Kingston Springs, TN 37082
(615) 952-5647
(615) 952-4934 FAX
Hand-hewn dovetail log and post and beam homes
Market area: Continental U.S.

Precision Craft Log Structures
711 East Broadway
Meridian, ID 83642
(208) 887-1020
(800) 729-1320
(208) 887-1253 FAX
Market area: Worldwide

Rapid River Rustic, Inc.
P.O. Box 8
Rapid River, MI 49878
(906) 474-6427
(906) 474-6500 FAX
Market area: Worldwide

🌲 Real Log Homes
National Information Center
P.O. Box 202
Hartland, VT 05048
(802) 436-2121
(800) REAL-LOG
(802) 436-2150 FAX
Market area: U.S. and export

🌲 Rocky Mountain Log Homes
1883 Highway 93 South
Hamilton, MT 59840
(406) 363-5680
(406) 363-2109 FAX
Market area: Worldwide

🌲 Satterwhite Log Homes
Route 2, Box 256A
Longview, TX 75605
(903) 663-1729
(800) 777-7288
(214) 663-1721 FAX
Market area: U.S., Japan, Mexico, Europe

Shawnee Log Homes
Route 1, Box 123
Elliston, VA 24153
(703) 268-2243
Market area: U.S., Canada, Middle East, Far East

🌲 Southland Log Homes
Route 2, Box 1668
Interstate 26 at Exit 101
Irmo, SC 29063
(803) 781-5100
(800) 845-3555
Market area: United States and export

🌲 Stonemill Log Homes
7015 Stonemill Road
Knoxville, TN 37919
(615) 693-4833
Market area: Continental U.S.

🌲 Tennessee Log Buildings, Inc.
P.O. Box 865
Athens, TN 37303
(615) 745-8993
(800) 251-9218
(615) 744-8156 FAX
Market area: Worldwide

🏠 Timber Log Homes
639 Old Hartford Road
Colchester, CT 06415
(203) 537-2393
(800) 533-5906
(203) 537-2438 FAX
Market area: East of Mississippi River

🏠 Town & Country Cedar Homes
4772 U.S. 131 South
Petrosky, MI 49770
(616) 347-4360
(616) 347-7255 FAX
Market area: Worldwide

🏠 Ward Log Homes
P.O. Box 72
39 Bangor Street
Houlton, ME 04730
(207) 532-6531
(800) 341-1566
(207) 532-7806 FAX
Market area: Nationwide

Wholesale Log Homes, Inc.
P.O. Box 177
Hillsborough, NC 27278
(919) 732-9286
(919) 731-9302 FAX
Market area: Eastern U.S. and export

Wilderness Log Homes, Inc.
Route 2
Plymouth, WI 53073
(800) 852-5647 (WI)
(800) 237-8564 (U.S.)
Market area: Worldwide

Wisconsin Log Homes, Inc.
2390 Pamperin Road
P.O. Box 1105
Green Bay, WI 54307
(414) 434-3010
(800) 678-9107
(414) 434-2140 FAX
Market area: Nationwide

Woodland Homes, Inc.
P.O. Box 202
Lee, MA 02138
(413) 623-5739
(413) 623-5556 FAX
Market area: New England and eastern NY

Yellowstone Log Homes
280 N. Yellowstone Road
Rigby, ID 83442
(208) 745-8108
(208) 745-8110
(208) 745-8525 FAX
Market area: U.S. and Japan

2. Panelized Building Systems Council, Post and Beam Builder Members

Some manufacturers of post and beam or timber houses are members of the Log Homes Council; others are members of the Panelized Building Systems Council (PBSC) of the National Association of Home Builders. However, not all members of the PBSC are manufacturers of timber or post and beam houses, so we have attempted here to provide a list that includes only timber or post and beam home manufacturers.

Modern post and beam houses are built in the style of the old post and beam houses that were popular in early America, but incorporate today's technology and energy efficiency.

If a timber or post and beam house appeals to you, contact one of the following manufacturer members. The listings also include the market area covered by each company, for your convenience.

Cedar Forest Products Company
107 W. Colden Street
Polo, IL 61064
(815) 946-3994
Market area: Nationwide

Classic Post and Beam Homes
P.O. Box 546
York, ME 03909
(207) 363-8210
(800) 872-BEAM
Market area: Worldwide

Forest Home Systems, Inc.
RD #1, Box 131K
Selinsgrove, PA 17870
(717) 374-0131
(800) 872-1492

Harvest Homes, Inc.
1 Cole Road
Delanson, NY 12053-0189
(518) 895-2341
Market area: NY, VT, MA, CT, NJ, NH, PA

Hearthstone, Inc.
Route 2, Box 434
Dandridge, TN 37725
(615) 397-9425
(800) 247-4442
Market area: Worldwide

Lindal Cedar Homes
Box 24426
Seattle, WA 98124
(206) 725-0900
Market area: Worldwide

New England Homes, Inc.
270 Ocean Road
Greenland, NH 03840
(603) 436-8830
Market area: ME, NH, VT, MA, CT, RI

Timber Truss Housing Systems, Inc.
525 McClelland Street
Salem, VA 24153
(703) 387-0273
Market area: Virgina and export

Timberpeg
P.O. Box 474
West Lebanon, NH 03784
(603) 298-8820
Market area: U.S., Japan, Canada, Caribbean, England

Woodland Homes, Inc.
P.O. Box 202
Lee, MA 02138
(413) 623-5739
Market area: New England and eastern NY

Yankee Barn Homes, Inc.
HCR 63, Box 2
Grantham, NH 03753
(603) 863-4545
(800) 258-9786
Market area: Nationwide

3. Hearth Products Association Members

Henry Thoreau, he of the different drummer, once said: "Possibly from the accidental discovery of the warmth of fire, and the consequent use of it, at first a luxury, arose the present necessity to sit by it." Approximately 78 percent of American home buyers include a fireplace or wood-burning stove as a preferred option. Following is a partial list of manufacturers of fireplaces and wood stoves, taken from the Membership Directory of the Hearth Products Association (HPA). To shop for a fireplace or a wood stove, first check the Yellow Pages of your phone book under "Fireplace Equipment — Retail" for the names of dealers near you. If you are having trouble locating a dealer, contact one of the manufacturer members listed below for the name of a dealer near you.

Aladdin Steel Products, Inc.
401 North Wynne Street
Colville, WA 99114
(509) 684-3745
(509) 684-2138 FAX

Appalachian Stove & Fabricators, Inc.
329 Emma Road
Asheville, NC 28806
(704) 253-0164
(704) 254-7803 FAX

Austroflamm U.S.A., Inc.
30518 Huntwood Avenue
Hayward, CA 94544
(510) 475-2690
(510) 489-8419 FAX

Conlen Industrial Corporation
1637 Billy Casper Drive
El Paso, TX 79936
(915) 598-6550

The Country Iron Foundry
83 Chestnut Road
P.O. Box 600
Paoli, PA 19301
(215) 296-7122
(215) 644-0367 FAX

Country Stoves, Inc.
P.O. Box 987
Auburn, WA 98071-0987
(206) 872-9663
(206) 931-1271 FAX

The Earth Stove, Inc.
10595 Southwest Manhasset Drive
Tualatin, OR 97062
(503) 692-3991
(503) 692-6728 FAX

Energy King — Manufactured by
Chippewa Welding Inc.
Route 5, Box 190
Chippewa Falls, WI 54729
(715) 723-0277
(715) 726-1080 FAX

England Stove Works, Inc.
P.O. Box 206
Monroe, VA 24574
(804) 929-0120
(804) 929-4810 FAX

Fabco Fireplaces
P.O. Box 340
Eagle, ID 83616
(208) 939-8218
(208) 939-1454 FAX

Fireplace Manufacturers, Inc.
2701 South Harbor Blvd.
Santa Ana, CA 92704
(714) 549-7782
(714) 549-4723 FAX

Fireplace Supply, Inc.
12700 N.E. 124th Street, #10
Kirkland, WA 98034
(206) 821-4800

Fuego Flame Fireplaces
P.O. Box 3551
2618 Ellington Road
Quincy, IL 62305
(217) 223-1642
(217) 223-1642 FAX

Grizzly Stoves-Derco Inc.
10005 East U.S. 223
P.O. Box 9
Blissfield, MI 49228
(800) 631-5538

GSW Heating Products Company
100 E. Wilson Bridge Road
Worthington, OH 43085
(614) 438-2636
(614) 438-7547 FAX

Harmon Stove & Welding, Inc.
352 Mountain House Road
Halifax, PA 17032
(717) 362-4251

Heartland Appliances Inc.
5 Hoffman Street
Kitchener, Ontario N2M 3M5
(519) 743-8111
(519) 743-1665 FAX

Heatilator Inc.
1915 West Saunders Road
Mt. Pleasant, IA 52641
(319) 385-9211
(319) 385-9225 FAX

Hi-Teck Stoves Inc.
2985 South 3600 West
Salt Lake City, UT 84119
(801) 975-0548
(801) 973-0506 FAX

Ithaca Manufacturing
1210 Avenue A
P.O. Box 78
Ithaca, MI 48847
(517) 875-4949
(517) 875-3699 FAX

Jotul USA, Inc.
400 Riverside Street
P.O. Box 1157
Portland, ME 04104
(207) 797-5912
(207) 772-0523 FAX

K & W Fireplace & BBQ
23107 Temescal Canyon Road
Corona, CA 91719
(714) 277-3300
(714) 277-2070 FAX

Long Mfg., Inc.
111 Fairview Street
P.O. Box 1139
Tarboro, NC 27886
(800) 334-5622
(919) 823-4151 FAX

The Majestic Company
1000 East Market Street
Huntington, IN 46750
(219) 356-8000
(219) 356-9672 FAX

Malm Fireplaces, Inc.
368 Yolanda Avenue
Santa Rosa, CA 95404
(707) 523-7755
(707) 571-8036 FAX

Martin Industries
P.O. Box 128
Florence, AL 35631
(205) 767-0330
(205) 740-5192 FAX

Napoleon Fireplaces — Wolf Steel
Rural Route 1, Highway 11 & 93
Barrie, Ontario L4M 4Y8
CANADA
(705) 721-1212
(705) 722-6031 FAX

Orrville Products, Inc.
375 East Orr Street
P.O. Box 902
Orrville, OH 44667
(216) 683-4010
(216) 684-2691 FAX

Osburne Manufacturing Inc.
555 Ardersier Road
Victoria, British Columbia V8Z 1C8
CANADA
(604) 383-6000
(604) 382-4128 FAX

Piazzetta S.P.A.
Via Montello 22
Casella D'Asolo, 31010 .
ITALY
(423) 950 350
(417) 55178 FAX

Rinnai America Corporation
1662 Lukken Industrial Drive W.
LaGrange, GA 30240
(404) 884-6070
(404) 884-6099 FAX

Royal Crown European Fireplaces, Inc.
333 East State Street, Suite 206
Rockford, IL 61104
(815) 968-2042
(815) 968-0739 FAX

Russo Products
61 Pleasant Street
Randolph, MA 02368
(617) 963-1182
(617) 961-1777 FAX

Rustic Crafts Co., Inc.
P.O. Box 1085
Scranton, PA 18501
(717) 969-1777

Schaefer Company
601 N. Long Street
P.O. Box 1716
Salisbury, NC 28145-1716
(800) 888-7092
(704) 637-0091 FAX

Scott Stoves Inc.
P.O. Box 1033
Hayden Lake, ID 83835
(208) 772-7310

Sherwood Industries Ltd.
6820 Kirkpatrick Crescent
Victoria, British Columbia V8X 3X1
CANADA
(604) 652-6080
(604) 652-0567 FAX

Summit Stove Company, Inc.
1330 North 131st Street
Seattle, WA 98133
(206) 362-2133
(206) 362-6567 FAX

Superior Fireplace Company
4325 Artesia Avenue
Fullerton, CA 92633
(714) 521-7302
(714) 994-6821 FAX

Teton Stove Company, Inc.
489 Edwards Road
Narvon, PA 17555
(215) 752-8300

Travis Industries, Inc.
10859 117th Place Northeast
Kirkland, WA 98033
(206) 827-9505
(206) 827-9363 FAX

Vermont Castings, Incorporated
Prince Street
Randolph, VT 05060
(802) 728-3181
(802) 728-3940 FAX

Waterford Irish Stoves, Inc.
16 Airpack Road, Suite 3
West Lebanon, NH 03784
(603) 298-5030
(603) 298-7885 FAX

Wet Industries, Inc.
14601 Arminta Street
Van Nuys, CA 91402
(800) 824-5550
(805) 521-1018 FAX

Wilkening Fireplace Company
HCR 73
Box 625
Walker, MN 56484
(218) 547-3393

The foregoing list of manufacturers is courtesy of:

Hearth Products Association (HPA)
1101 Connecticut Avenue, NW, Suite 700
Washington, DC 20036
(800) 942-2887

For more information on pellet-fired appliances (PFA's), send a self-addressed #10 envelope to:

Fiber Fuels Institute
5013 Miller Trunk Highway
Duluth, MN 55811

4. Floor Plans

Craftsman 1600

This smaller home, with abundant grace and charm, works a lot of living into a compact floor plan. The main level features a formal entry, a quiet den or parlor, a large kitchen and dining room, and a formal living room with cathedral ceiling; the porch off the dining room is perfect for alfresco dining.

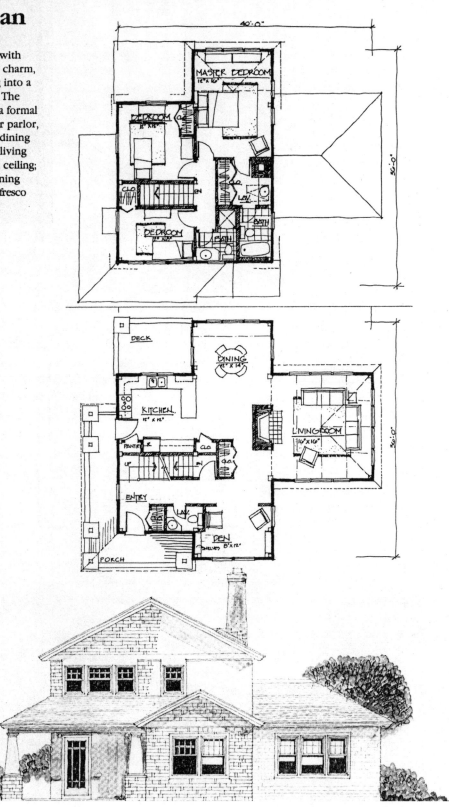

Craftsman 2600

A mid-sized, family home with ample living areas that flow together gracefully. The sunken living room and library add a touch of formality; the porch is accessible from both the dining and living rooms; upstairs, all bedrooms have generous closets. *The garage shown is optional.*

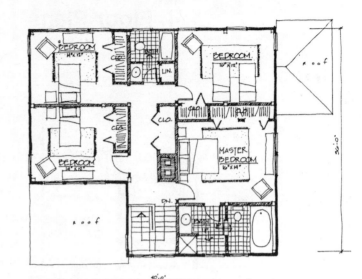

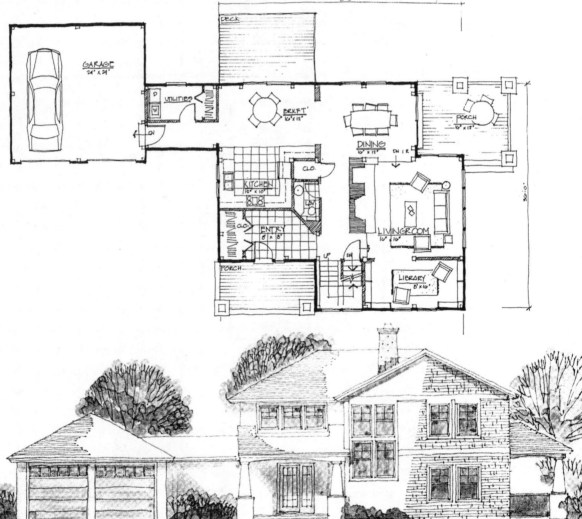

Craftsman 2800

This home is similar to the Craftsman 2600, but most of the rooms have been expanded. French doors divide the formal entry from the foyer; the expansive kitchen area includes both breakfast and family spaces; and the dining deck can easily be modified to serve the family and breakfast rooms. Upstairs, a balcony overlooks the grand stairway. *The garage shown is optional.*

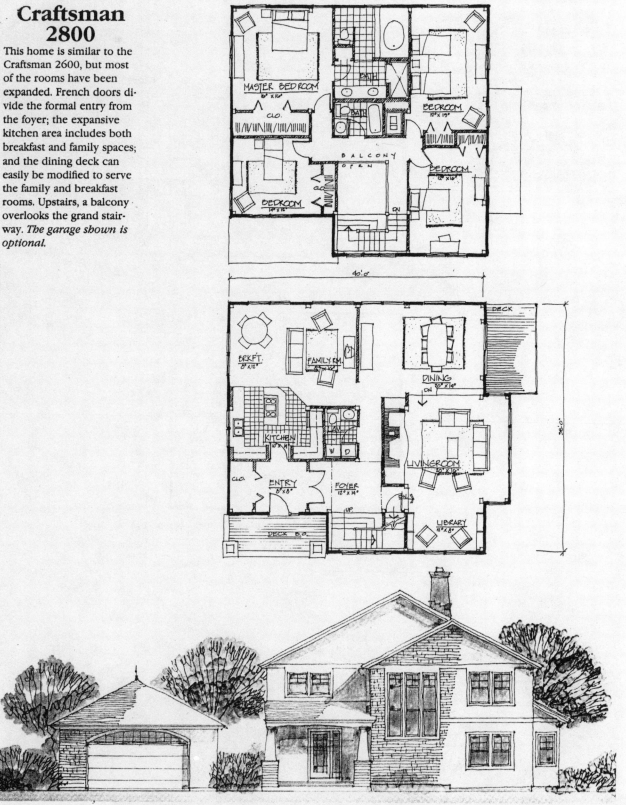

Nantucket 1800

This home is designed "up-side down," to take full advantage of the views and breezes. The bedrooms are on the first floor, the living areas are on the second floor, and a ladder leads to a third-floor loft space with built-in bunk beds.

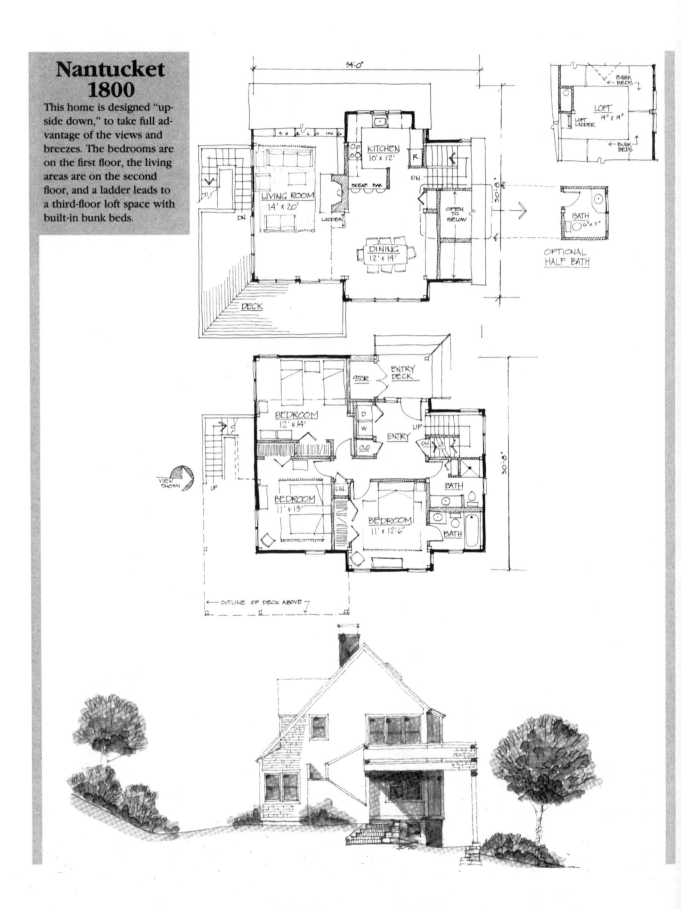

Galena 2200

Compared to the Nantucket 1800, this home has a larger and more traditional floor plan; it also has a more contemporary exterior style. The kitchen and dining room have access to a porch, which can easily be screened in for comfortable outdoor dining; there is also a large deck, which expands the living room space; and the cozy den can double as a guest room. The third floor has a large loft space; the optional lower level (not shown) provides space for additional bedrooms or an activities area.

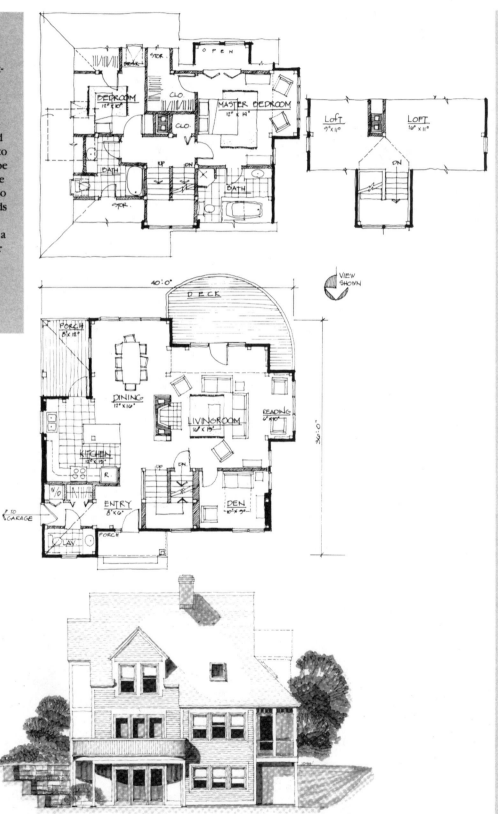

Hartland 2400

A variation on the Galena 2200 with the same overall dimensions—but more living space. The kitchen, dining room, living room and office are each distinct rooms; the living room has a larger cathedral area; the deck has been moved to join with the porch; and there is now a third bedroom on the second floor.

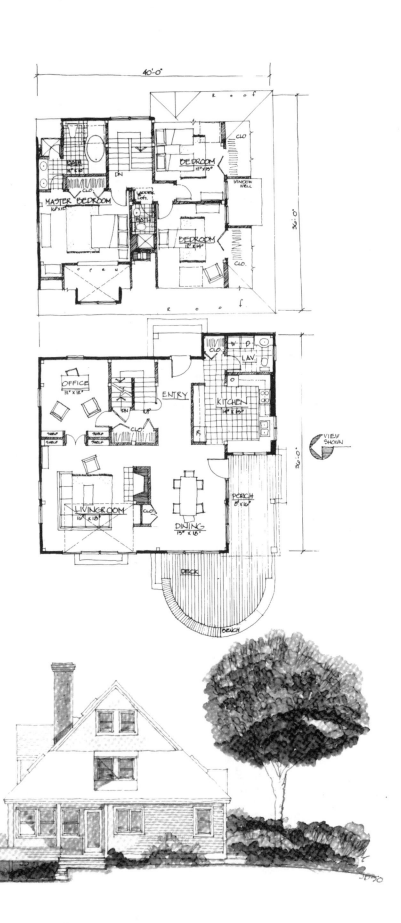

Aspen 2200

This compact home is a perennial customer favorite. The lower-level walkout area (not shown) can have a family room or possible bedroom and bathroom; the first floor features a relaxed floor plan with a den or bedroom; there are two second-floor bedrooms, and a third-floor loft (not shown).

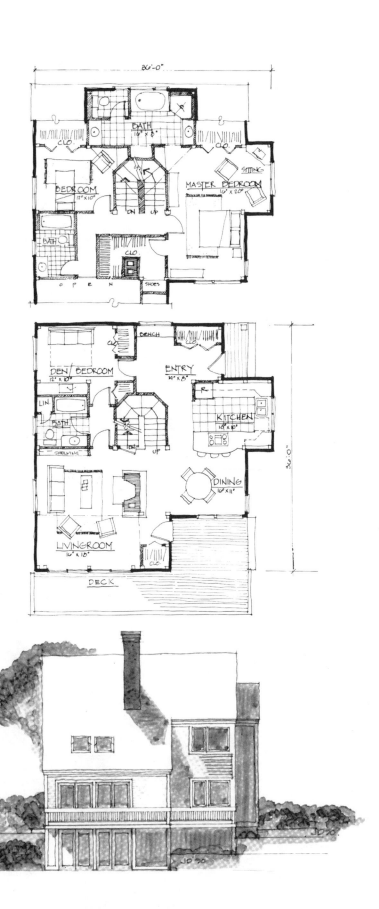

Hanover 2350

Perennially popular, this home includes all the amenities of a family-oriented floor plan; spaces flow easily from room to room, and subtly combine informality with just the right amount of formality. Special features include an upper-hall window seat, a master bedroom fireplace, and a large mud room/laundry with plenty of space for boots, coats and sports equipment; two of the bedrooms have ladders leading to their own private lofts; and for additional storage, this house has an old-fashioned attic.

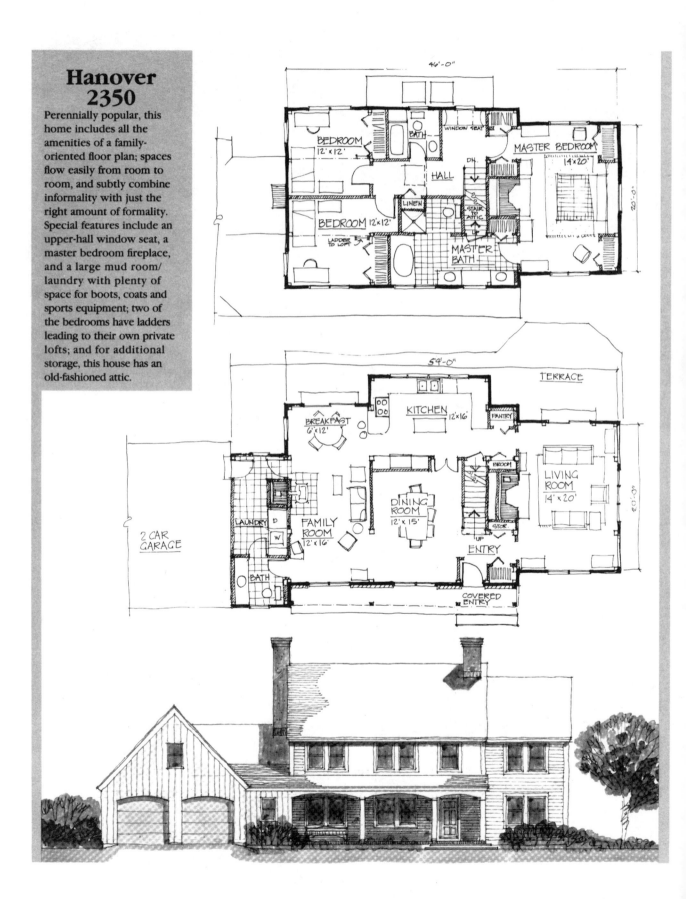

Essex 2400

An exceptionally spacious, modern floor plan in a moderately sized, tradition-ally shaped package. This home lends itself very well to either authentic or con-temporary decoration, and features a third-floor loft.

LOFT
16'0" X 13'0"

MASTER BEDROOM LOFT

DN.

OPEN TO BELOW

DECK

BREAKFAST
8' X 12'

DINING
12' X 12'

LAUNDRY

BATH

KITCHEN
12' X 12'

DN.

UP.

LIVING ROOM
12' X 22'

STUDY
10' X 10'

ENTRY

80'-0"

OPEN TO BELOW

STORAGE

BEDROOM
10' X 11'

BATH

CLO.

BATH

STAIR HALL

MASTER BEDROOM
12' X 14'

BEDROOM
10' X 11'

DN.

UP.

LINEN

80'-0"

Dover
2200

This style of home has been familiar in the mid-Atlantic region for many years. The smallest wing could be expanded slightly to accommodate an additional first-floor bedroom; each second-floor bedroom features a private bathroom. *The garage shown is optional.*

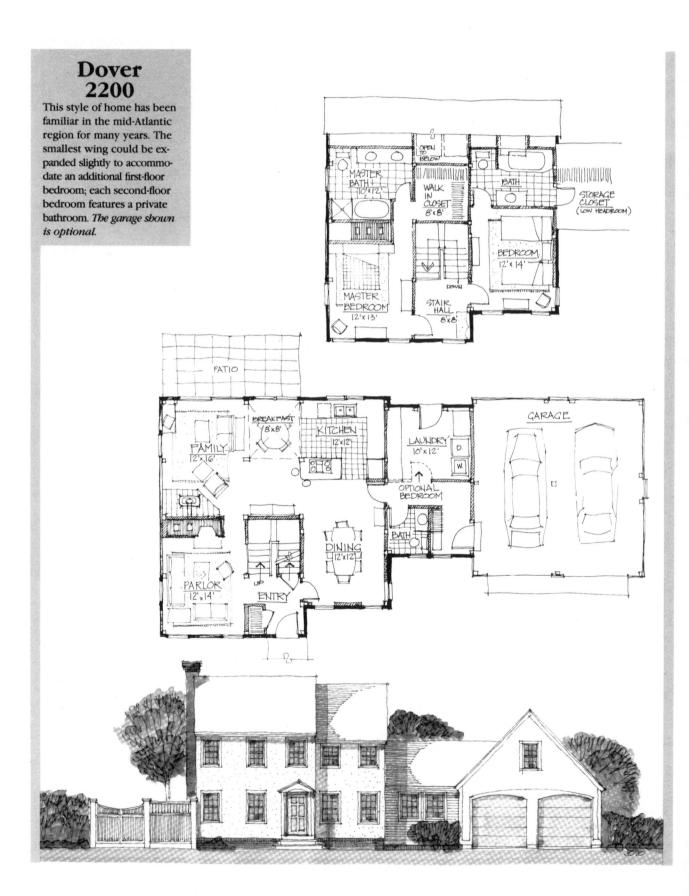

Mediterranean 2000

With its very broad roof overhangs, this home is perfect for even the warmest climates; and because of its single-level plan, all the rooms have cathedral ceilings. As shown, this home has been modified to accommodate the needs of a person in a wheelchair—note the wide doorways, ramps, handrail bathrooms and turnaround spaces. (The garage shown is optional). Many Timberpeg homes are easily adaptable to design considerations such as these; if you have special needs for your home, please speak with your Timberpeg Independent Representative.

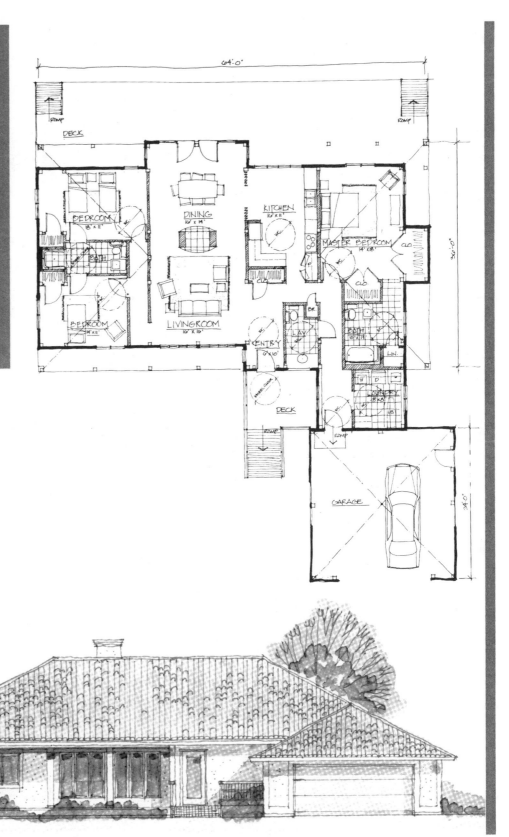

Gambrel 2400

A popular home with an expansive, open feeling. The kitchen, dining room, family room and living room all flow gracefully together, and both the dining and living rooms open onto a recessed porch—a perfect area for comfortable chairs. The entire living room has a cathedral ceiling, and there is plenty of room for built-ins; the office would make an ideal guest room.

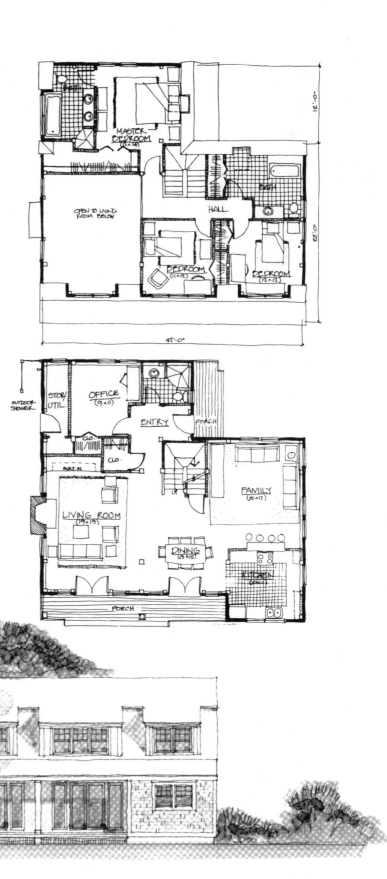

Gambrel 2475

This home has a more formal room arrangement than the Gambrel 2400, and somewhat smaller exterior dimensions—but it still has plenty of efficient living space. The reduced cathedral area and absence of a porch help make this a more economical home to build.

Gambrel 2500

What sets this home apart from Gambrels 2400 and 2475 are its private deck off the master bedroom, and the addition of a fourth upstairs bedroom. Downstairs, it has a sunken living room with sun room addition, and both the kitchen and dining room open onto a porch, for easy outdoor meals.

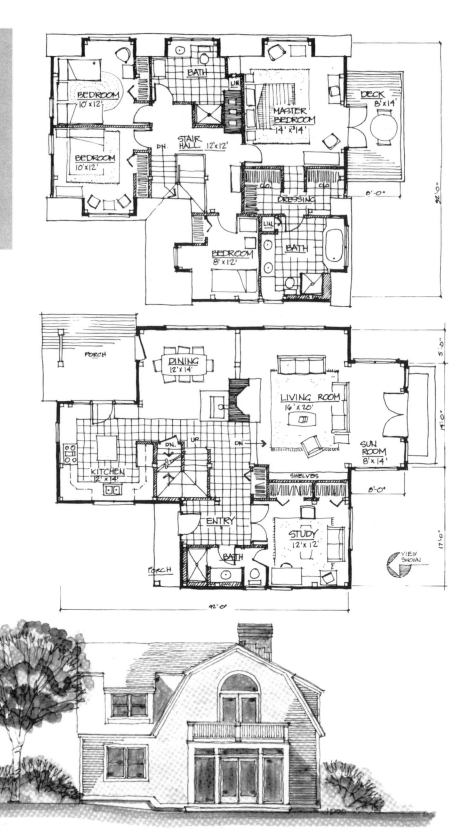

Country Living 1700

This is the original *Country Living* model: compact in size, open in plan, economical to build, and oriented toward a primary view. It features an efficient kitchen with plenty of storage, a dining room with a skylit cathedral ceiling, and a den which may serve as a guest room—and which also has double doors that may be opened to expand the generous living room. The master bedroom has quite an interesting cathedral ceiling and a spacious outdoor deck.

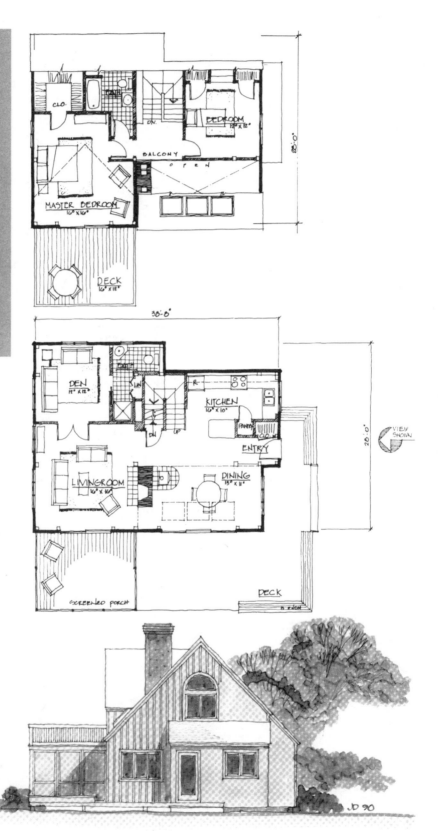

Country Living 2000

A slightly expanded variation of the Country Living 1700, with a more formal entry and the inclusion of a laundry and mud room. Each upstairs bedroom has a cathedral ceiling and its own private bathroom, and the master suite has a large walk-in closet.

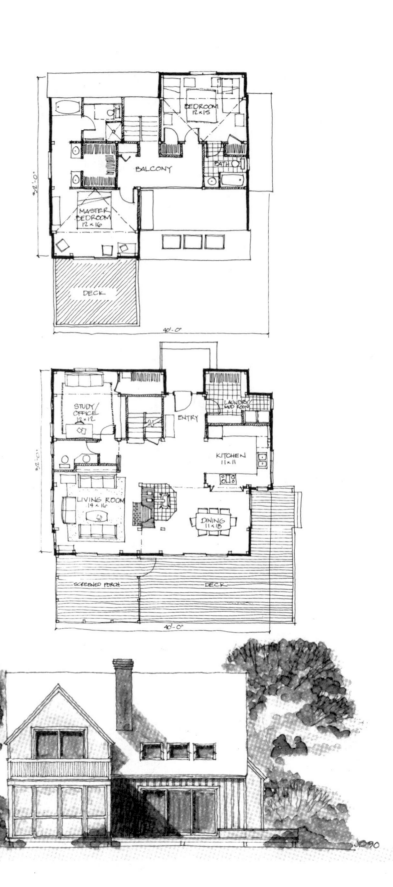

Country Living 2001

This Country Living home features an additional bedroom and bathroom, a gourmet kitchen, and a larger living room. *A garage and airlock entry are optional.*

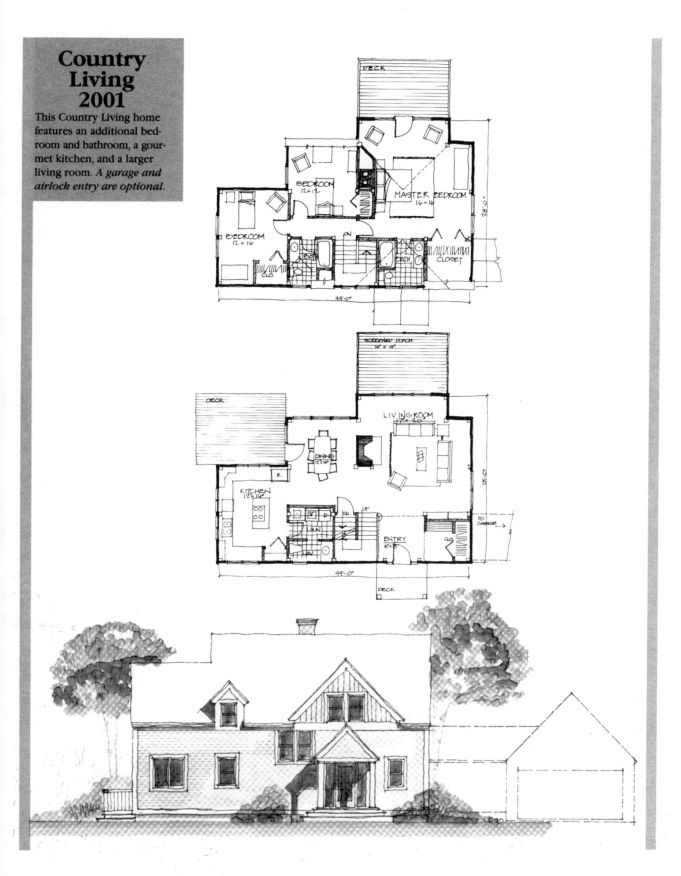

Hatteras 1500

This coastal cottage makes a wonderful beach home. Porches surround the home almost entirely; there is a screened porch for comfortable outdoor meals, and a convenient outdoor shower.

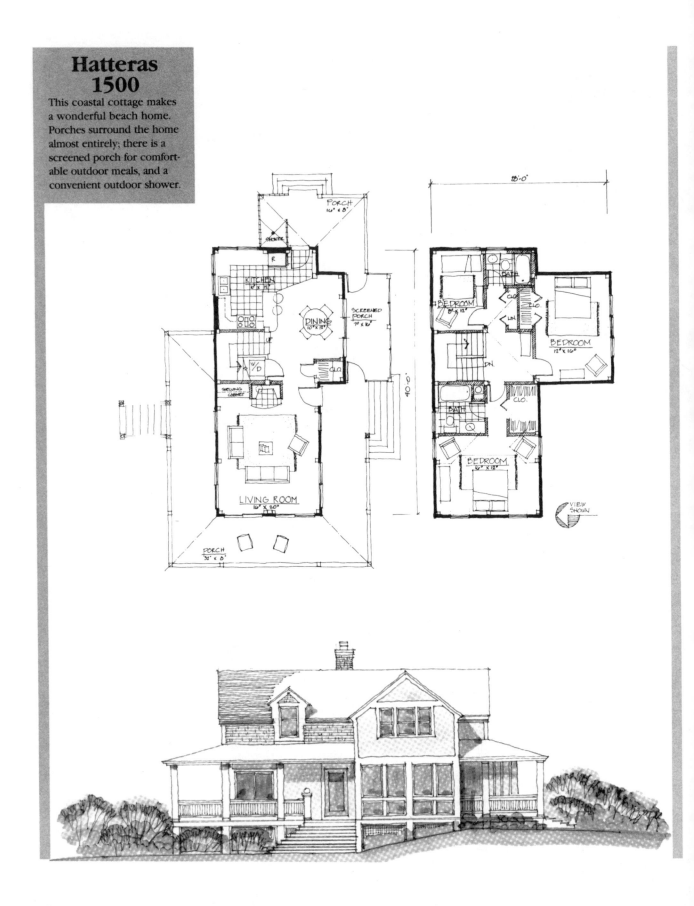

Gardener's Cottage 1800

Classic symmetry is the key to this design. The living room, dining room, kitchen and entry are all arranged around a central staircase and hearth; outside, there are twin porches for dining and lounging; both upstairs bedrooms and bathrooms are surprisingly large.

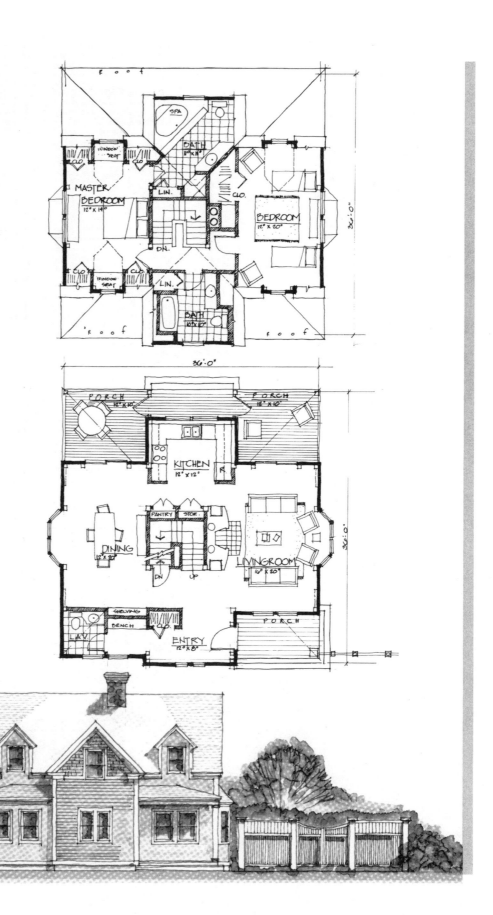

Rutherford 4400

This large home has a room arrangement and exterior style with the flavor of a Northern Italian villa. The private office, or library, has direct outside access, and is especially well suited for a professional working at home. Upstairs, the two main bedrooms both have vaulted ceilings, and the grand master suite—which could easily include a fireplace—features its own exercise room. There is also a convenient upstairs laundry and work area. *The garage shown is optional.*

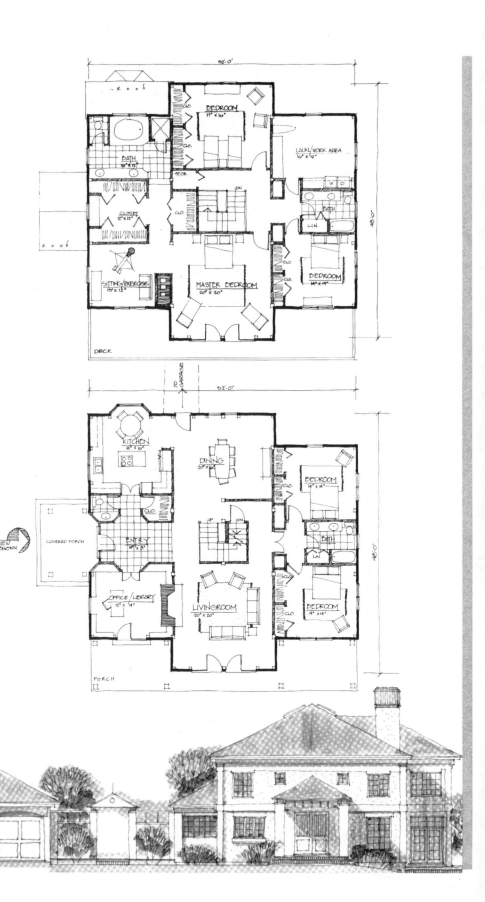

Sanibel 1700

A perfect warm-climate home based on a classic Florida belvedere design. Raising the home off the ground improves ventilation, protects against rising water, gives excellent views, and also provides convenient parking space. Each of the corner rooms has a cathedral ceiling, and the lanai, decks and porches (shown here with screens) virtually double the living area; a fireplace can easily be added. The upper-level belvedere (not shown) provides added ventilation, and may be used as an observation area or quiet retreat.

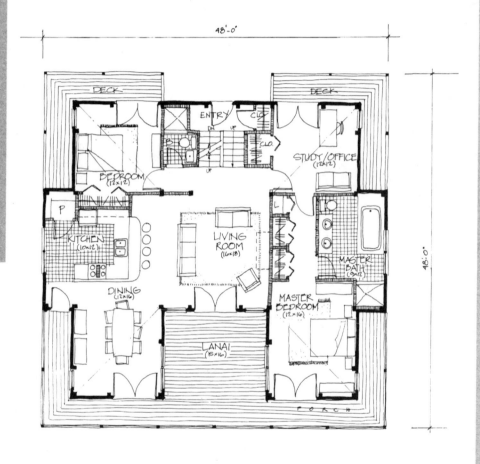

Carefree Cape 1600

This small design includes many desirable features not normally found in a home of its size: a formal entry, a kitchen with breakfast bar, an enclosed sun space, and a living room with a cathedral ceiling and fireplace. For economy, the upstairs may be left unfinished (or finished at a later date), and the study area can become a comfortable master bedroom suite. *The garage shown is optional.*

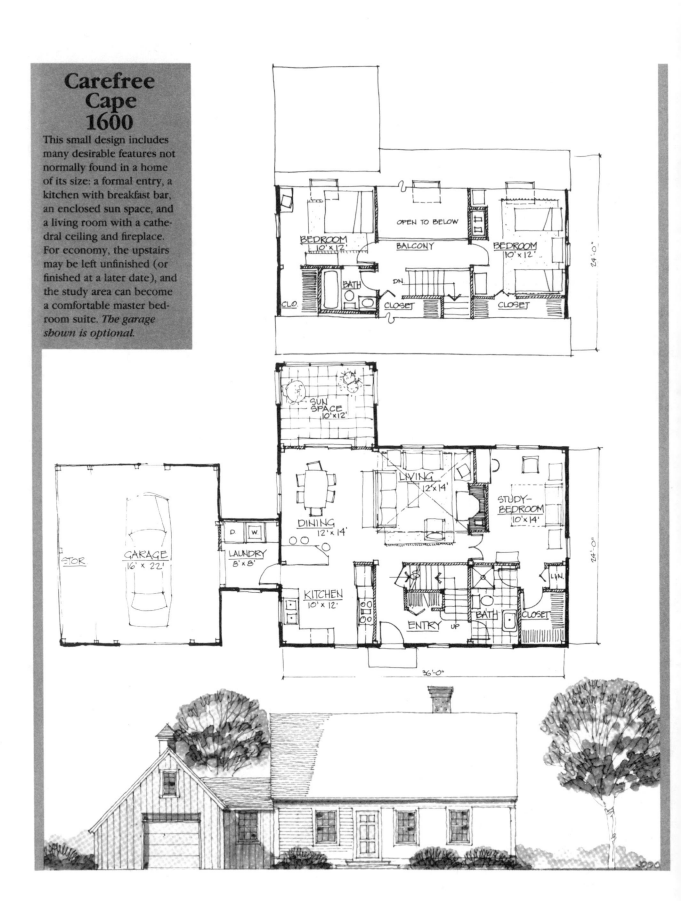

Carefree Fairway 1000

Whether you build it as an expandable starter home, a place for easy getaways or a home to retire to, this efficient, single-level design has no compromise on quality or charm. The kitchen and great room areas have cathedral ceilings, while the bedrooms have flat, plaster ceilings (built with conventional trusses). The overall design and shape make this one of our most economical homes to construct.

Carefree Fairway 1000A

In this alternate floor plan of Carefree Fairway 1000, we've slightly rearranged the rooms. If no third bedroom is needed, the walls can easily be eliminated and the living room expanded. *The floor plans shown here are just two suggestions for this home; your Timberpeg Independent Representative can discuss other possibilities with you—including a plan with a stairway to a lower level.*

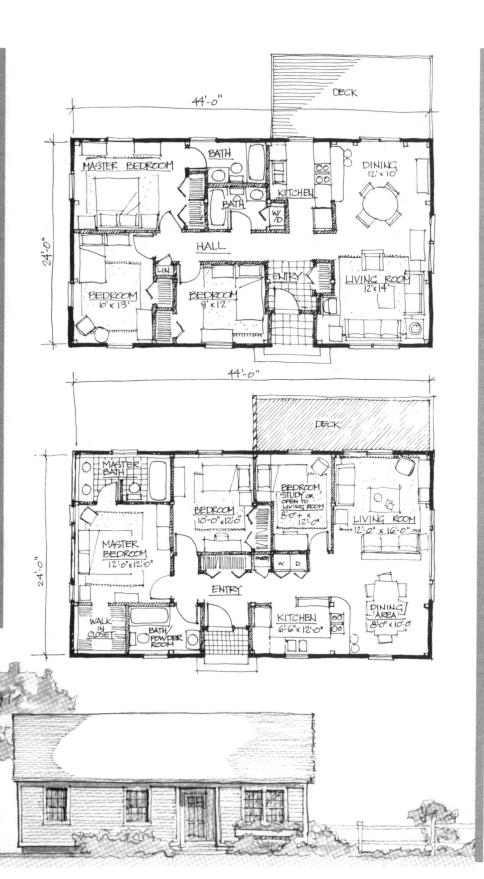

Avon 2800

A mid-sized, family home perfect for occasional entertaining on a small to medium scale. The family areas are to one side, the formal areas are to the other, and the two are joined by a deck that runs the entire length of the home. The living room has a vaulted ceiling, and the spacious master bedroom suite has its own sun deck.

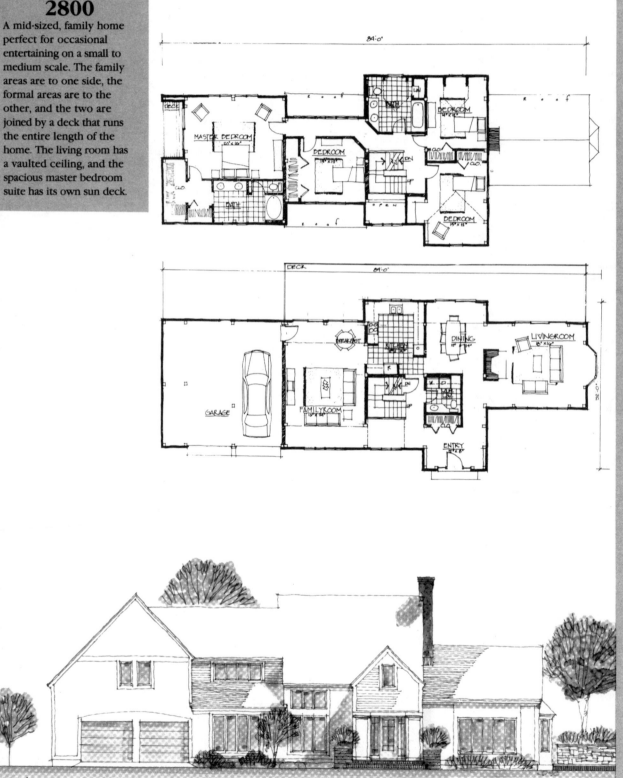

Newtown 3300

A classic American home that includes many of the features families want most: a formal entry, formal living and dining rooms, a large kitchen, sun-filled breakfast area with an adjacent family room and deck, and an efficient laundry and mud room. There are three generous bedrooms on the second floor—including a master suite with a sumptuous bathroom—and an activity room or office with its own separate entrance; there is also a large loft space on the third floor (not shown).

Fairfield 3200

This home is similar to the Avon 2800, but the rooms have been rearranged in an open plan that is marvelous for large gatherings; the home is also designed to take wonderful advantage of an expansive view. It features a skylit, two-story grand entry; a very large kitchen with generous counter space and a cozy window seat; an enormous great room with a wet bar, cathedral ceiling and skylights; and—as a quiet sanctuary from the rest of the house—a living room that can be closed off behind French doors. The master bedroom suite has a large, private deck.

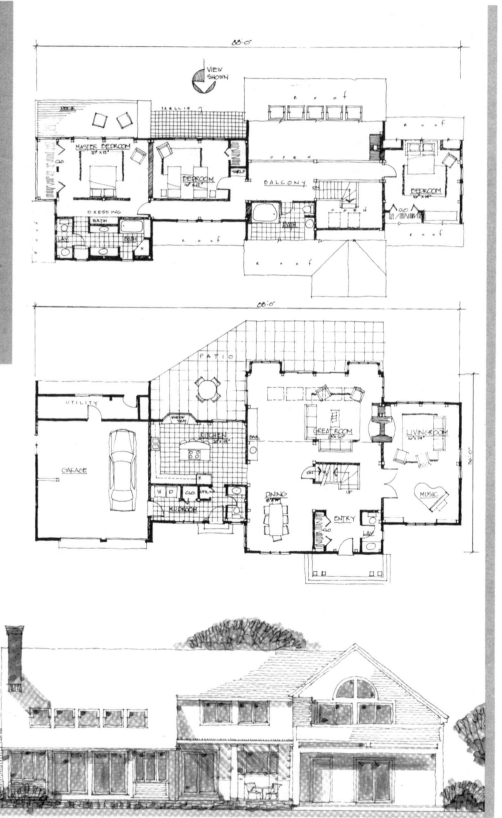

American House
Princeton 2900

An informal, open plan and ground-hugging design make this home reminiscent of a rambling American farmhouse. The elegant first-floor master suite has a cathedral ceiling, a separate office or library, and a private deck for sunning. The upper-level bedrooms surround a large, open play area; a lower level (not shown) can accommodate additional bedrooms or an activities area. *The garage shown is optional.*

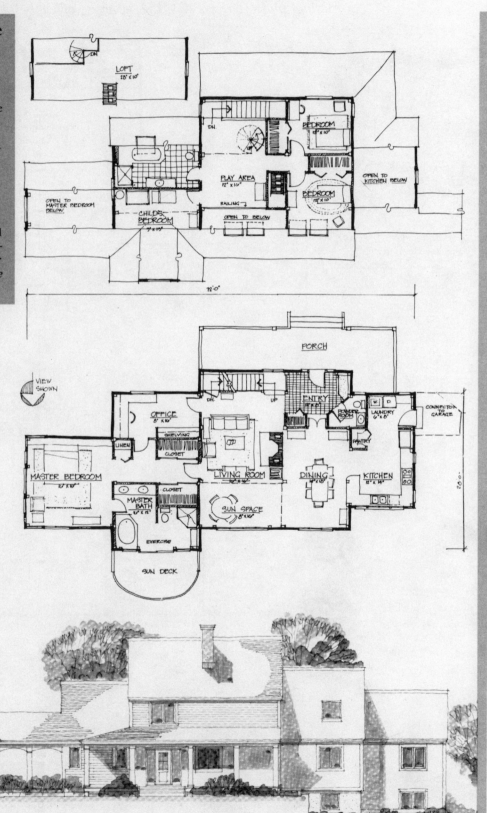

All floor plans (pages 127 – 154) courtesy of Timberpeg.

American House
Lakewood 2600

With its defined but flowing living areas, this home offers a variety of entertainment options inside and out. For comfortable living year-round, there is expansive glass to the south, a greenhouse, and a screened porch. The second floor has three bedrooms, and the third floor has two large loft rooms.

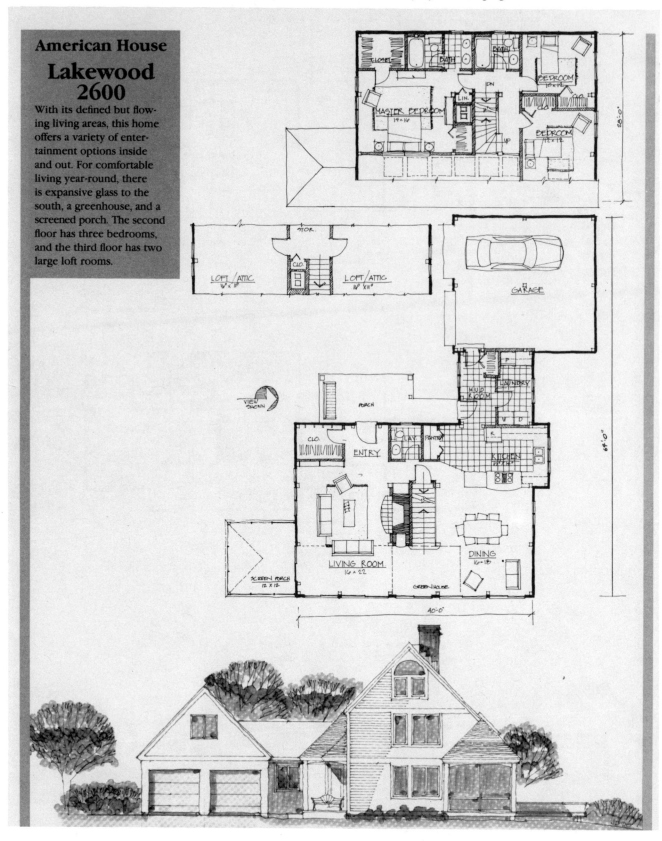

Index